D0260663

The Confident Fly Fisher

Cunliffe R. Pearce

The
Confident
Fly Fisher

ADAM & CHARLES BLACK
LONDON

FIRST PUBLISHED 1972

BY A. AND C. BLACK LIMITED

4, 5 AND 6 SOHO SQUARE, LONDON, WIV 6AD

© 1972 CUNLIFFE R. PEARCE

ISBN 0 7136 1270 3

All rights reserved.
No part of this publication may be reproduced,
stored in a retrieval system, or transmitted,
in any form or by any means, electronic, mechanical,
photocopying, recording or otherwise,
without the prior permission of
A and C Black Ltd.

Printed in Great Britain by Billing and Sons Limited
Guildford and London

Contents

PART VI   OTHER WAYS

PART VII   EXPERIENCE

Illustrations

Acknowledgements

I am very grateful to my friends William Watson and Tom T. Robertson, for the diagrams in the text: and to the editors of *Trout & Salmon* and *Rod & Line* who have kindly given me permission to use articles originally printed in their journals.

[1]
Introductory

As no man is born an artist, so no man is born an angler.

IZAAK WALTON

Angling is somewhat like poetry, men are to be born so.

IZAAK WALTON

Recently a friend of mine decided to take up trout fishing as from his fiftieth birthday. For thirty years his hobby had been social work which, with a good conscience, he now relinquished to younger men. Deliberately he chose fishing as the recreation of the second half of his adult life because he judged it, after careful consideration, the ideal activity. It offered an absorbing interest, with rich intellectual and literary associations which were essential to his particular predilections; reasonably strenuous exercise in the open air for the sake of his health; mild excitements suitable to his temperament; and something else, less easy to define. More and more as the years went by he had become aware of a strange, almost primitive, feeling which many simple people make no secret of, but which tends to be educated out of men of his attainments or only to be confessed in certain recognised situations such as the casino or the racecourse—the very Greek feeling that human life, however complicated, however sophisticated, is still influenced by the goddess of fortune. He laughs and calls this the *oracular appeal*. When he has consulted the oracle, taken the omens, read the auspices, he is readier for the decisive actions of life. Fishing for him is the perfect oracular appeal. When he comes back from a successful day by the river he is top-sides with the world. Strange to say, even an empty bag is not always failure. It is a sign that fortune's favours are not cheaply earned. Better preparation, more care, greater skill are demanded of him. It is a lesson applicable not just to his fishing but to his other more important affairs as well; it is a lesson he learns over and over again. In two years of fishing he has discovered more about life, so he says, than in half a lifetime. Yet he is still very modest, perhaps rightly so, about his fishing; for his greatest achievements are only occasional half-pounders which he thanks the goddess for. In his other affairs, which his fishing allegedly improves, he is making a considerable name for himself.

Obviously this man was not born an angler. He is a remarkable learner who came to it by deliberate choice rather late in life, instead of, like many of the rest of us, at the obscure bidding of instinct in childhood or early youth. What he has done others may do.

Though, like many other superstitions, the use of fishing as a form of appeal to fortune comes from deeper regions of the psyche, it does not constitute him a born angler. I am sure there *are* born anglers whose motivations are all deep ones. The pleasures they discover along the way, however genuinely felt, are only rationalisations for their choice of sport. They usually begin early in life, only needing opportunity which they seize by instinct, as we say. Many writers have, rather facilely, identified specific instincts of which the so-called hunting instinct is the most popular. I don't quarrel with this theory: it would indeed be surprising if, after millions of years' evolution as a carnivorous hunting animal, man did not have a strong in-built tendency of this sort. But instead of trying to identify instincts in man, which are not unlike myths, I think we can learn more by examining the very real physiological influences on our behaviour. For example, eyesight.

Much has been written about the eye of the trout and the importance of the trout's vision for angling methods. The eye of the angler has been strangely neglected. The very fact that fly fishing involves a long-sighted hunter pursuing a short-sighted prey is a matter of interest. Furthermore, eyesight is distributed among the total human population in the ratio two to one: there are twice as many long-sighters as short-sighters. This must be biologically satisfactory for the human race and has been determined by ages of evolutionary process. Both kinds of eyesight are good, but good for different things. The hunter, the sailor— all who tend to be interested in the horizon and far-off things— have long-sight. The craftsmen, the weapon makers and, in more recent times, the readers and writers of books, find short-sight more satisfactory.

I am arguing that eyesight determines our life style. A slight difference, barely one thirty-second of an inch on either side of the norm, in the size of that precise and very uniform organ, the human eyeball, makes for long- or short-sight: and this difference is given by heredity. Among children, whose eyes have not reached mature size, long-sight is much commoner than among adults. Thus it is that boys will take to fishing enthusiastically before about age fourteen, who after that age, when their true form of vision begins to make its influence felt, experience a considerable change of interest; not just in fishing, of course. Nevertheless, our crowded river banks are a good indicator of the preponderance of long-sight among the population as a whole. If only nature had arranged things differently; if only the statistics of long- and short-sight had been the other way round, the number of anglers would be halved and the fortunate long-sighters would have room to cast their flies. Idle wishes.

There is a practical side to this subject. Beginners should be aware of what angling requires. No doubt short-sighters, if they are determined, willing to put up with difficulty and disappointment, will get some satisfactions: like Andrew Lang, who confessed himself a hopeless duffer, who only once in his angling career ever saw a trout rise to his fly and yet persisted all his life in the sport he so astonishingly loved.

It would be a kindness, at least, to warn, if not warn off, short-sighted acolytes. Fortunately this is seldom necessary: for it is true, we choose our way of life, for the most part, unconsciously, at the bidding of our physical endowment. Not we but our eyes choose for us. Short-sighted persons tend not to go in for fly fishing. There are so many different forms of angling that almost any kind of physique can be satisfied. Even blindness has not proved completely inhibitory, though it almost certainly rules out fishing with the dry fly.

One event which may happen to any of us is sheer tragedy. The most poignant chapter in angling literature known to me is Viscount Grey of Falloden's *Retrospect* to the 1930 edition of his famous book, *Fly Fishing*, in which he sadly bids goodbye to the sport he had enjoyed and adorned throughout a distinguished life. There was no cure then for his failing sight. He describes the stages of decline. In 1918 he found he could no longer descry his fly on the water, a serious handicap to a dry-fly fisher. In the following season he was unable to see the rise of a trout. Downstream wet-fly fishers may think sight less important for their craft, but Grey did not find it so. We use our eyes so habitually as to be unconscious of the extent to which we are dependent on them. Finally, the only fly fishing left to Grey was for salmon, and even here the affection of the central area of his vision made only limited success possible for a season or two until at last he had no prospect but only a lifetime of retrospect to enjoy.

So far I have been trying to justify and reconcile Izaak Walton's inconsistencies, which seem to me both understandable and endearing. The quotations from *The Compleat Angler* at the head of this chapter, taken individually, as one finds them in that wonderful book, ring true. Juxtaposed, they are clearly contradictory. Perhaps truth always behaves like that. Walton, at any rate, was of two minds about anglers and, rather belatedly, I am coming to his rescue. It seems likely that there are two sorts of anglers, the born and the made. Aptitude and natural skill are not to be denigrated, and no doubt born anglers are closer to tradition and folk ways; they seem less inclined to read books, more conservative in their methods. Whereas, in my experience, the made angler is more consciously desirous of help and instruction and likely, therefore, to adventure farther into modern methods. In this scientistic or technological era, the more deliberately one chooses a way of life the more one can exploit the knowledge and inventions that are accumulating. Perhaps there is also a between-angler, one who keeps all options open, making the most of what nature and science offer him. This is the whole case for education—and for the writing of books on fishing.

But not everyone wants to take up fishing, and there are many reasons for not doing so, some of them as deep-seated as those that impel others to fish. Among the disincentives are scruples about the killing of trout which is still, though it may not always be, a detail of the sport. Trout fishers don't want the killing aspect exaggerated because they judge it a small part of the whole proceeding. Small, but not unimportant. Women are, perhaps understandably, more deterred by it than men. As yet few women fish for trout, perhaps because trout are relatively small fish. Women are proportionately more numerous among salmon fishers, either because salmon are larger and therefore less disturbing of their feminine sensibilities, or else because the gillie usually relieves them of the unpleasantness. Killing apart, fly fishing for trout would seem ideally suited to women, being gentle, clean, graceful—in a word, aesthetic. There are signs that women are discovering this.

The killing of trout is important because angling is not a cruel sport. There are cruel anglers, just as there are cruel people anywhere. Killing fish is not the object of the sport, which is an innocent recreation pursued for the sake of the many pleasures that accompany it. It so happens that trout are considered good to eat and they are given a quick and merciful death to that end. Unless one is a genuine vegetarian he has no case against the killing of trout by anglers. Cruelty, of which the non-killing of captured fish might be a serious instance, is not a feature of trout fishing that should cause concern to reasonable people, at least as long as the vast net-fishing industry, the broiler-houses, and the abattoirs that the modern world requires, continue to supply fish, fowl, and flesh for the carnivorous appetites of the human race.

I remember an incident of my boyhood. I was fishing Tweed where it flows through the public park at Peebles. I caught a trout and killed it. A man who was sitting on a seat watching me called out. "You should never do that," he said. "Killing the fish spoils its flavour." I was and remain horrified at such a cruel notion. He went on to ask what fly I was using. I told him, Partridge and Yellow. He said I'd do better with a Black Spider. The two things remained associated in my mind for years. Although I learned to acknowledge the value of a Black Spider, I hated it and never used it because of the man who had offended my sense of right and wrong.

I conclude this rather serious discussion with William Scropes's classical reply to those who accused him of following a cruel pastime: "I take a little wool and feather and make an imitation of a fly; then I throw it across the river. Up starts a monster fish with his murderous jaws and makes a dash at my little Andromeda. Thus he is the aggressor, not I; his intention is obviously to commit murder. You see then what a wretch a fish is: no ogre is more blood-thirsty, for he will devour his nephews, nieces, and even his own children when he can catch them; and I take some credit for having shown him up."

I write these pages towards the end of Conservation Year, 1970. A few words on this topic would be appropriate. At last we are all becoming apprehensive about dangers threatening the environment. This will surely result in measures to save it. The idea that angling is a threat to fish life in our streams and lochs is a very old one.

> *But now the sport is marred; and wot we why?*
> *Fishes decrease—for fishers multiply*
> ANON., 1598

It is not a just observation. On the contrary, angling improves the state of our waters in all important respects; for there are few fisheries that are not managed. Management varies greatly in efficiency for many reasons; but its overall effect is to provide more and better fish, living in purer and more plentiful waters than would be the case if angling demand was less than it is. If I encourage an increase in the number of anglers, I do so with a good conscience.

Anglers are naturally conservationist and in some areas seem to be the only public opinion against the evils of abstraction, pollution, and canalisation of streams. Management, of course, costs money, and angling on the cheap is not to be justified. Free fishing is not in itself an evil. The last trout will not be taken on a fly. But other evils are equally free where fishing is free; the inevitable result is a dearth not only of trout but of every other amenity associated with our waters.

Industrial development has extended its influences so widely that natural fishing for wild trout is unobtainable except in the remotest parts. Even there, where management may be relatively non-existent, conditions are seldom satisfactory. Waters that have plenty of good spawning grounds may be overstocked with starved and stunted fish. Where spawning opportunities, as well as food supplies, are scarce the trout may be large but few, and fishing for long wearisome hours to little purpose the inevitable lot of the angler.

The contemporary increase in the numbers of anglers, thanks to modern affluence and mobility, is a less serious threat in itself than its main effect. By the law of markets, available resources are being bought up by those who can most easily afford them. Salmon was always largely a rich man's preserve. Trout, especially in Scotland, was the democratic fish: that is, it was available very freely to the poorer members of the community. Sometimes one hears the cry: "Hands off our traditional freedom"; which ignores the accidental nature of that freedom. Unless proper measures of conservation are undertaken democratically, both trout and salmon fishing may become the privilege only of rich men or large business syndicates.

The time is ripe for more than discussion of these matters. Governments, concerned with the problem of leisure, which creates great expectations of popular happiness as well as frightening examples of anti-social misuse, are as much involved as the humblest citizen whose modest desire is to have an occasional day's fishing in pleasant surroundings. Legislation, such as that recommended in the Scottish Hunter Report, 1965, is required to ensure access for fishing to an adequate number of waters in every district, proportionate to the population or its demand, and to make provision for the financing of all the necessary management to preserve, fertilise, and stock the waters taken into public service. Anglers will have to pay for their sport and not cheaply: but they will be assured of a great increase of opportunity in all areas as well as improvement in the quality of sport provided. This will mean not loss of freedom but the price of opportunity. I am not a pessimist. I see a great future for angling. It depends largely on the wisdom and courage of anglers now.

PART I
The Trout

[2]

A Dish of Trout

... rose-moles all in stipple upon trout that swim.

GERARD MANLEY HOPKINS

If I catch a Trout in one Meadow, he shall be white and faint, and very like to be lowsie; and as certainly, if I catch a Trout in the next Meadow, he shall certainly be strong, and red, and lusty, and much better meat.

IZAAK WALTON

Sooner or later when his initial impatience has cooled, no doubt after he has acquired a stock of problems and some disappointment, the trout fisher will acknowledge it is the trout that determines methods of fishing for it. Its nature and habits are as important as tackle and technique. Some information, therefore, about the trout would logically come early rather than late even in a very practical book. The impatient reader is still free to please himself in what order he reads the chapters.

It is good practice to study your catch. I once examined a plate of five trout and tried to discover some relationship between what I saw and what I experienced in catching them. Their total weight was just two pounds, about average for the water they came from and fairly typical of the ticket waters the majority of anglers fish.

They varied remarkably in colouration. One was very dark. I caught it from a shady hole where the current flowed under a large tree, close to an undercut bank. It rose, nevertheless, to a floating fly. Although dark, it had large red spots. Another two were light coloured, iridescent, and speckled freely with small red spots. They both looked rather fat and were clearly in good condition. They too had been taken on dry fly, and I remembered with keen pleasure their extravagant jumping displays. Of the other two, which were both caught on sunk fly, one splashed all the way to the net, probably because I gave it no opportunities;

the other made the reel spin and, by getting deep into heavy water below me, gave me more concern than any of the others. To be just, I would have to judge this last as the liveliest of them all, though not lively in any spectacular sense. Before it came to the net I was sure it was a much bigger fish. Both these trout, caught on the sunk fly, had red spots, were light skinned, and well conditioned. I should add that I lost a nice fish which spurted out of the water in a high-flying leap the moment I struck at the rise and was off the hook before reaching the water again.

The main object of the exercise was to examine the question of liveliness. The trout is a very agile fish. It indulges in quite fantastic aerobatics and its playing is often a series of breath-catching emergencies. That is a principal reason for the sport of fishing for it. But its behaviour is not uniform. Somewhat reluctantly, after observing it carefully on many occasions, I have come to believe that how a trout fights has less to do with its essential liveliness and more to do with the angler's methods. Dry-fly fishing makes an especial appeal to many anglers for just this reason. It's the liveliest form of fishing. Everything happens on the surface. The fight begins there and, although a fish may take the hook down, more often than not its first flings are surface ones. Feeding on the surface, from a high lie, probably adapts the fish (by swim bladder adjustment) to operating in the higher layers. Fish that take worms or sunk nymphs will be more conditioned to the lower levels and tend to fight it out there. The question of liveliness, therefore, resolves itself into a comparison between two different kinds of fighting. The surface fighter will have all the appearance of being the livelier fish, which may not be a just observation.

A further interesting fact about liveliness may be mentioned. In waters shared by salmon and trout the angler should be able to distinguish between the smaller specimens of each species. The salmon, at least, will have to be returned. Very early in my fishing I learned, infallibly I believe, to know the difference between a parr and a trout by their different behaviour. When a small fish is hooked, if the angler shortens line and then lifts it by hand, so that the fish is suspended, he will know at once what it is by the wriggling. One fish has a slow swinging type of wriggle or else it hangs without struggle. The other's is an unmistakable, short-wave, high-frequency one, a vigorous head-body-tail vibration. I never need to distinguish the two by any other sign. The trout fisher, whose partiality is for his own fish, will perhaps be disappointed to learn that the salmon parr is the livelier performer. This must be significant: perhaps it has to do with the greater need for fast acceleration to enable the salmon to surmount obstacles on its spawning run. However, this is the only respect in which the trout's liveliness need be qualified.

Its muscular body is made for vigorous turning. Compare a grayling and a trout in the hand. The one has large scales and its body feels stiff. The trout's scales are small and, though not limp, its body gives a feeling of lusty flexibility. This suits it admirably to the fast turbulent waters it mostly inhabits. From its feeding lie it can move rapidly upwards or to either side to intercept its prey and return to position by a single, powerful body-tail thrust without being swept away by the force of the water. For economy of effort its lie will be where the forces of the current make it easy to maintain position. In fact, it will be almost held in position by water pressure. Any movement out of its lie must be quick enough to involve the minimum expenditure of effort, in overall terms less than the value of the food so obtained. This turning power makes it well adapted to surface feeding.

When a trout goes off with the hook, when the reel sings and the line cuts through the water, the angler gets an impression of great speed. Actually it is known that trout swim at a speed of eleven or twelve knots, maintained for a comparatively short distance. Acceleration in the first few yards may attain twenty knots. Attached to a line its speed will be even less. The angler's rather exaggerated impression is a consequence of surprise, the noisy spinning of a narrow disc, and the rapidly diminishing sense of control as the line extends. Ten yards rapidly taken out puts a very anxious distance between him and the trout. Of course, a false impression does not detract from the satisfaction of the experience.

My plate of trout has other lessons to teach. One is the extreme colour variability of this fish. At one time as many as twelve separate species of brown trout were recognised. Today there is almost unanimity. *Salmo trutta* is a single species. Even the sea-trout belongs to it. But the trout varies in so many ways that it is customary to use a variety of names in popular speech—brown trout, Loch Leven trout, sea-trout, gillaroo, etc. Even from the same water, individual fish of a catch may seem very different from each other, not only in size, but in colouration and other respects. My plate of trout did not give all the variations possible even for the water they came from. For instance, all of them had red spots, varying only in size and intensity. Red spots and pink flesh often go together and are believed to be due to the same ingredient of diet, namely, carotene. Waters rich in hard-backed food, such as snails and shrimps, produce trout with pink flesh and vivid red spots. Where this diet is deficient, trout tend to be whitefleshed and may have few, or small red spots, or only black ones. Because of variations in the food supply in different parts of a water, or because of selective feeding habits, which we shall notice later on, even a water rich in carotene food may produce white and pink, red- and black-spotted fish. There may also be seasonal variations in this respect. Whatever their colour, which may vary between black and red, the spots differ also in shape and size. Round, starry, or haloed spots may be distinguished. Science has not yet accounted for these differences.

There is a strong prejudice in favour of the higher colouration which is supposed to go with enhanced palatability. My study of the five fish I have been telling you about ended with a postscript: "All the trout on the plate seemed equally appetising. Unfortunately none was red-fleshed." Obviously, therefore, colour of spots and flesh may be different, though it would be guess-work to theorise about the cause.

I took my five trout from a rough, rain-fed river. It flows over rock and fairly stable gravel in its different parts. The gradient is steep and the stream strong and broken at the head of each run. There are here and there slower flats where the bed becomes smoother and where, in winter, the grayling are often to be found. Coarse fish could subsist in these quieter reaches but are not encouraged by the management. Elsewhere the rock and stony gravel acquires a mossy felt which provides no shelter for the trout but ample protection for a great variety of insect life on which the trout mainly subsist. In most summers a fair growth of long streaming weed, mostly milfoil and ranunculus, attaches itself to the stones and is usually controlled by the periodic spates. The trout's richest food supply comes from the stony, mossy areas. Although the streamers add some variety, they serve the trout mainly for shelter, giving very satisfactory lies in the channels they create in the stream and adding to the vicissitudes of fly fishing. I like these weedier stretches, when a hot summer hasn't made them excessive, just because they multiply the lies and distribute the fish more evenly in the river.

The banks of such a river may not be so well cared for as those of the classical chalk stream. Anglers make a path through the vegetation so that access is reasonably easy in most parts, but untrimmed bushes and trees, shaggy and sometimes steep banks—hazards such as these make special demands on the angler's casting skill. Add a strong or gusty wind and the usual advice to the apprentice to practise casting on a lawn before going fishing seems almost ludicrous. Fishing here *has* to be learned the hard way, though practice in easy conditions is not wholly excluded. On such a river wading is almost necessary and greatly simplifies the approach problems.

This is a very typical trout water for which the trout is suited by nature. It is rich in food (especially so if it flows over calcareous rock somewhere in its upper course) and also in food-gathering lies, and has a great variety of other features. No single method of fishing would sufficiently exploit its opportunities, though the several branches of fly fishing give very adequate variety of technique and over the season prove more consistently successful. On other waters, especially perhaps the gentler, clearer, cool, spring-fed streams that come from the chalk, although other methods would not be impossible, they are less appropriate and possibly disallowed by the rules. Here fly fishing comes into its own. The chalk streams are of special interest in connection with this chapter because they have served as the scientific angler's laboratory, giving him excellent opportunities to observe and experiment.

At this stage a special word would be useful about two related requirements of the trout: its oxygen need and the range of temperature within which it lives and grows most happily. In respect of these requirements the trout is a specialised fish. Though it can share with coarse fish waters that have higher temperatures and less oxygen than its natural habitat, the trout cannot breed there and in an exceptionally warm summer may have to migrate again or perish.

The trout is a fish of the nothern temperate regions, found originally in an area bounded on the south by the Mediterranean and on the east by the River Oxus, though colonising Britishers, determined to have their trout fishing wherever they chanced to go, have introduced and maintained it in many likely and unlikely places elsewhere in the world. It requires cold or cool water. Like all fishes, its body temperature is the same as that of its surrounding element. Although it becomes more active as the daily or seasonal temperature of the water rises, its increase of energy is limited by the lower oxygen content of the warmer water. There is clearly the possibility of relating the trout's appetite and feeding activity to the oxygen/temperature conditions of the water at different times: studies in this direction are proceeding, chiefly in connection with growth rates, but not yet easily assessed by the angler for his immediate use.

Temperatures between 9° and 19° C produce greatest growth, optimum energy output being around 12°. Daily fluctuations from morning to evening, variations between shady and open water, effects of sun and cloud, all play a part. The angler has always tried to take such factors into account when fishing. The scientist may soon persuade him to use thermometer and oxygen-meter (but someone will have to invent it first). Salmon anglers have used the former for a long time now; so this kind of development would not be out of tradition.

[3]

The Trout's Senses

Look, what they lack in hearing, is supplied unto them in seeing chiefly.
ANON. *The Arte of Angling,* 1577

. . . advise Anglers to be patient, and forbear swearing, lest they be heard and catch no Fish. IZAAK WALTON

The trout is an unspecialised carnivore. That, in the language of science, tells us it eats anything alive. The obvious inference is that the angler must at all costs offer the trout living food or its simulation. The appearance of life is the first essential. Artificial flies must behave as do the real insects, which is a difficult requirement and has exercised the ingenuity of fly tiers from earliest times. The method of fishing, the presentation and working of the lure, is one sort of technique. The materials used, mobile hackles, translucent silks or furs, iridescent or reflective tinsels, etc, etc, have been put into service because mobility of limb, translucency of body, light-reflecting chitin or air bubbles adhering to the body hairs, are all features of insects that trout eat and as such are indicators of life. Almost any new development or fashion in the making of artificial flies has some connection with this paramount requirement. New modern synthetic materials promise an exciting period of experiment ahead of us: but the principle behind it all goes back to the earliest folk tradition of fly tying, the simulation of life and liveliness, and with few exceptions the very best answers to the problem, even the very materials recommended, are to be found in the recipes of the earliest experimenters. W C Stewart, author of *The Practical Angler,* whom I would describe as the inheritor of the folk tradition and one of its most articulate voices, is still essential reading on this topic a hundred years after his death.

The trout's feeding habits will concern us right through this book. It feeds at all levels, which makes for variety of fishing method. It feeds periodically according to appetite and opportunity. This presents special problems to the angler. Sometimes the river appears dead, with no sign of fish activity, which is very discouraging to beginners who are often, therefore, advised to begin on the smaller streams where, because of a comparative scarcity of food, trout tend to feed more continuously or at every opportunity. In another chapter I intend to deal with the taking times of trout, a knowledge of which will help to reassure the angler who begins to suspect a river is empty because nothing happens. Daily and seasonal variations in its appetite and feeding habits are necessary knowledge for confident and successful fishing.

This periodicity in feeding is further complicated by the habit of selective feeding which can infuriate any fisherman and completely bewilder the beginner. Again this is a commoner experience on the larger waters, though it can occur anywhere. Why should the trout behave so selectively in its attitude to the food available? No certain answer is possible. One is tempted to assert that, like ourselves, it gets a special liking for particular tastes at particular times. *Chacun à son goût*, however, hardly applies when every trout on the rise seems to have the same obsession. As a creature of instinct, it may be selecting items that make up for dietary deficiencies in its previous food supply. More likely it is just economy of effort. Where a variety of choice presents itself, olives and iron blues, for instance, at the same time, it may go for the one or the other because a repetition of the same minimum movement suffices. To alter its mode of attack repeatedly to suit both insects would be wasteful of effort when a single species is available in sufficient quantity. When a multiple choice is possible and the angler's observation or trial-and-error tactics prove completely unsuccessful, it is understandable that he is inclined to attribute it to the trout's sheer contrariness. It's part of the sport's fascination, nevertheless.

A short introduction to the trout and its habits can make no claim to completeness. Only some of the more determining characteristics of its nature and behaviour can be dealt with. A serious fisher would do well to find out all he can, for knowledge is seldom wasted: it will contribute to his practical efficiency as well as provide him with relevant interests.

I have left to the end of this section the most important topic of all, namely, the senses of trout and how they assist or frustrate the efforts of the angler. Two senses predominate, the vibratory sense, and sight.

Over the surface of the skull and in a line (really a channel of fluid with apertures through the scales to the outside) along each side of the trout's body is located an organ sensitive to vibrations in the water and perhaps also to pressures. In co-operation with the sense of sight it enables the trout to locate itself in the stream with constant awareness of water movements, neighbouring objects such as rocks, bank or weed beds which influence water movements, and perhaps also the nearness or approach of other fish. I would consider it the principal sense organ. Without it, the trout could not exist at all. I think, too, that it is especially important to the trout because of the active conditions of its habitat.

The lateral line, as this sensory apparatus is called, detects low-frequency vibrations in water. In its evolution the trout does not seem to have found any need for the detection of those high-frequency vibrations we call sound. True, it has ears, but concerned almost wholly with the sense of balance. Taking all these facts into consideration, the angler is clearly warned about how he moves near where he wants to fish. Clumping about the bank, carelessly scraping the rocks with tackety boots, or sending bow-eaves ahead of him as he wades is very likely to alert or frighten his timid quarry and prevent him getting anywhere near enough to have any hope of catching it. Apart from these kinds of disturbance it's more a matter of personal preference. By all means let him "Be quiet and go a-angling"; but if he wants to shout to the fellow on the other bank or even relieve his feelings by swearing at him, in spite of Izaak Walton's opinion, it won't make the slightest difference to his sport, except in so far as it may induce an unfavourable state of mind.

Sight is the second most important sense organ. The trout is a visual hunter. Smell and taste may play some small part at the moment of seizure, making possible very prompt rejection of mistaken samples of the "living drift" on which it mostly subsists. This speed of rejection is a special problem in all methods of fly fishing and raises nymph fishing to the rank of the most difficult form of all. But sight is certainly the trout's main instrument in the hunt for food.

For short distances it is very acute. The eye has a fixed focus lens but is capable of some protrusion and lateral movement to increase the angle of vision which sweeps about 330° sideways and forwards under water, limited in range by the density or turbidity of the water as well as by the focal length of the eye. Thus the trout, when stationary, has a blind area of about 30° backwards which allows the angler useful opportunities of undetected approach in an upstream direction as is specially recommended for fishing with the floating fly or the sunk nymph.

Light and, therefore, shadow as well, penetrate through all areas of the surface, losing intensity, especially in the ultra-violet and infra-red parts of the spectrum, as it descends. Blue light reaches deepest. An effort of the imagination is needed to understand the kind of world in which the trout lives. The most surprising fact, becoming familiar nowadays to skin-divers, is that it is an upside-down world; for its ceiling is a vast looking-glass reflecting the river bottom, if it is near enough, and all its details. Objects in mid-winter or nearer the surface may even be seen double, directly by illumination and again reflected in the mirror overhead. This may be one of the reasons why this expert food gatherer sometimes makes mistakes, taking the reflection for the substance and giving false indications to the angler.

The looking-glass ceiling over the trout's head, if it were uninterrupted, would effectively confine its vision and interest to its own element. There would be no dry-fly fishing. Fortunately for both parties there is a hole in this vast mirror. It is suspended, as it were, immediately above the fish's head and is as large as the base of an inverted cone making an angle of some 97° with its eyes. It is known as the trout's window through which is possible direct observation of the outside world. Wherever the trout goes it carries the window with it like a halo. It diminishes in size but increases in transparency, always assuming the surface of the water is undisturbed, when the fish rises to the surface, and behaves in the opposite sense when it descends. Anything passing across this window will attract the trout's attention. When feeding actively on surface drift it normally sharpens its short-distance vision by poising as near the surface as possible. When floating food is scarce and appetite still strong the trout lies deeper so as to observe a wider area of surface and not lose too many opportunities. If the surface is agitated by wind or current the window

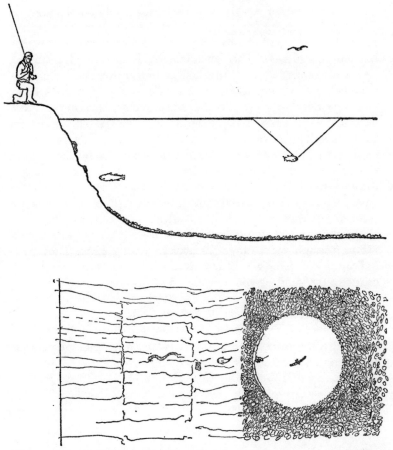

Fig. 1 Trout's Window showing the cone of the trout's clear vision through the surface. Everything below the surface, sufficiently illuminated by the prevailing light conditions, will be reflected up into the surface mirror all round the window.
Of the outside world only the bird overhead and the angler on the periphery will be seen by the trout.

becomes frosted or shattered. Objects may still be detected through it but more in silhouette and errors of detection will be more possible. In such conditions the angler's floating fly, if it has the visual form of a real fly and makes the same kind of impressed pattern on the surface tension, will be most likely to deceive the fish.

Finally, a further word about the trout's outlook through its window. Because of the difference between the refractive indices of air and water, the trout's cone of vision widens as it passes beyond the surface. This phenomenon is illustrated from the opposite point of view by the well-known apparent bending of a stick below the point where it enters the water. Hence the trout sees a wider world above the surface than one might have expected. A wag might say it sees round corners. The angler on the bank will not always be out of the line of the trout's sight when he thinks he is. As against this, objects nearer the horizon of the trout's view will appear much smaller than those seen straight through the middle of the window. Nevertheless, anglers who have advantaged themselves by thus diminishing their image, especially if they move about or attract attention by reason of alertingly bright clothing, may be just as frightening. The trout's vision, though short range for acuity, is long enough for such indications of danger. Objects on the surface passing across the centre of the window will increase up to full size before diminishing again. This is the case with a well-placed floating fly.

"I have an ambition", wrote Charles Cotton, "to be one of the greatest deceivers," defining in these few words the whole immoral purpose of fly fishing. To succeed in his ambition an angler must have some understanding of the trout's sensory apparatus so that, by taking advantage of its limitations, he may entice his victim into a last and fatal error of judgement.

[4]

The Trout's Larder

The grand mistake of all the authors I have seen on fly fishing is their supposition that the flies are alighting on the water from above, whereas, could they catch up the idea, or be persuaded when told, that the flies arise to the surface from the bottom where they are bred, sheets of useless speculation might be saved.   JOHN YOUNGER, 1840

A trout fisher should always be asking questions. Where? how? and what? are the three most important and best asked in that order, because skill of presentation, that is, the accurate placing of his flies where the fish will see them, is the first requirement. At the waterside the commonest question is, no doubt, "What's the fly?" but that assumes the other two have already been answered. A wrong fly well presented has a good chance of attracting a feeding trout, whereas the right fly incorrectly placed may escape notice altogether or only succeed in making the fish suspicious. Thus the arrangements of the trout's larder are more important than its contents.

The trout lives in its larder. Some of its food is under the floor or in or above the ceiling, but most of it shares the watery space in between. In a river the larder is not static. It is a conveyor belt with a soft liquid underpart in which the trout roves or poises, ready for any food brought to it. Its lateral sense organ gives it constant awareness of movements in the travelling water so that any additions or alterations in its familiar rhythm or pulse are immediately detected, giving signals of danger, perhaps, to its timid mind or of food to its appetite. The small insects on which it mostly subsists are very unlikely to be noticed by the lateral organ, sensitive though it is. Even the drag of an artificial fly fished down and across stream will be seen rather than felt. Nowadays spinning lures, which perhaps always stimulated the lateral sense, are being specially designed for this very purpose;

C.

but the fly fisher is content to appeal only to the trout's sense of sight.

Most of the food under the floor is hidden. The trout is not specialised like certain coarse fish for foraging or rooting at the bottom. His attention is directed mainly in horizontal and upward directions. There are occasions when it stands on its head, "tailing" as we say, but then it is rummaging among the moss or weeds rather than into the actual bed. Since the bed of a typical trout stream is a cementation of rock this is not very surprising. Insects that live in the interstices are difficult to get at. Those that live on the floor itself protect themselves against discovery by camouflage, encasement, or slow movement. The trout gets his opportunities of these insects mostly when they change their positions in the larder, and his eyesight is sharpened for those occasions.

Bristle worms of various kinds inhabit the gravel, silt, or mud of the slower reaches. These worms and the larvae of dragonflies and Mayflies come to the trout's notice most often when the bed is violently disturbed. The periodic floods of the rain-fed river do this and also give the trout experience of other food creatures washed into the stream from the banks. I used to wonder at the effectiveness of worms as trout bait until one day when I caught a trout in a subsiding river. As I took it, rather clumsily, from the net it disgorged a walnut-sized lump of small worms, many of them still alive, on which it had obviously been feeding liberally. If all trout in that well-stocked water had been eating worms at the same rate, the total number available must have been in the millions range. Trout don't need anglers to introduce them to worms. Similarly, insects that live under stones are not normally available to the trout unless they emerge from shelter or are washed out of it in special circumstances which are common enough.

Some insects eaten by trout are wholly aquatic, but those that concern the angler most spend the earlier and longer part of their lives in the water and the remaining part in the air. During the course of their changing lives the trout gets few but, because of the vast numbers of insects involved, ample opportunities of capture, so that flies in their several stages provide a large portion of its food. The eggs of these aquatic insects are deposited on or near the bottom, or sink to it by gravity from the surface. The larvae that emerge from the eggs have various habits; they may burrow, crawl, or swim. The burrowers, as we have seen, are for the time being out of the trout's reach. The crawlers hide among the stones or so protect themselves that they too are fairly safe. The swimmers or darters dodge in and out of rocks and weeds, thereby encouraging the trout to hunt them, but are only marginally more accessible. The time comes, however, for all of them to change their life style and situation in the larder. This gives the trout its best opportunities.

As they grow the larvae frequently moult, each time shedding their inelastic and now inadequate outer skins. Twenty-nine such moults have been observed in a single experimental case which may or may not be exceptional. It is not known for certain how frequently such moults are assisted by temporary migrations into the upper layers of the water. Some insects may make visits to the surface to take in air to assist the shedding of their disused husks. What is certain is that at the final moult of the larval stage, when the insect has developed its wings under the carapace of its thorax, it rises or swims to the surface preparatory to leaving the water altogether and becoming a winged fly. This is likely to be the most vulnerable time of its life. It is of mature size, its wing case is very conspicuous, and the surface tension of the water may actually hinder its emergence to the air. The trout take a heavy toll of these "hatching" flies.

The fisherman's name for a fly in its larval stage is nymph. Nymphs live in water for the greater part of their lives; one, two or more years. Their dangerous migration to the surface may be only a matter of a few moments in each case: the trout's main chance, therefore, is a small proportion of nymphal time. It is uncertain what conditions determine the rise of nymphs. Particular times of day or season for particular insects become familiar to the experienced angler. For instance, the March Brown emerges, in spite of its name, sometime in April; the Mayfly, as its name suggests, towards the end of May. Other insects such as the Large Spring Olive or the Iron Blue Dun, may begin to appear early on and continue at intervals thereafter for the rest of the season. Some have two times of emergence, in spring and again in autumn. Undoubtedly temperature of water and air affects mature nymphs and helps to induce their hatching response. Amount of light and length of day may have something to do with it. Fly hatches are common, or so anglers often think, in certain conditions of atmospheric pressure, though what effect this could have under water is not easily explained. A familiar feature of the nymphal rise is its mass nature. It may take place at the same time all over the water, sometimes for miles in any direction, which indicates general causes. On other occasions it may be more localised. What the fisher sees is the effect of a rise of nymphs on the trout, especially in the latter stages of the rise when they may show considerable excitement as they attack nymphs in the surface skin or newly emerged duns in the act of drying their wings as they float on the surface—a "boiling rise".

It seems, therefore, that a rise of trout which excites the angler is only in a secondary sense a matter of the trout's behaviour. The real cause of a "rise", as the angler calls the whole pheno-menon, is not the decision of the trout to come on the feed, but the consequence of an upward migration of mature nymphs which arouses, or gives opportunity to, the trout's appetite. Apart from the common mass rises, the trout seems to have other fairly frequent chances of taking nymphs in the upper layers of the water during much of the daylight hours. This more casual feeding may be due to temporary migrations of younger nymphs, as already noted, to final migrations of older individuals, or to nymphs dislodged from their usual positions and set adrift in the current. Waterlogged winged insects may also form part of the drift available for hungry trout poised on the lookout.

The middle layers of the larder are the most heavily stocked. The roof, which is penetrable, sometimes with difficulty, by the insects and easily by the agile trout, provides second and third opportunities. This is when its attention is directed upwards to the mirror and, more especially, to the window. Any creatures caught in the membrane of the surface are easy prey. The mem-brane usually assists the hatching process, holding in its grip the old husk out of which the fly can climb, extracting its wings, limbs, and body so quickly that the angler is amazed to see a fly pop out, as it were, from nowhere in the blink of his eye. But sometimes a puff of wind may heel the fly over on its side: if a wing touches the skin of the water it adheres at once, and the fly is doomed to drowning or capture by a trout.

As a rule, however, the fly erects its wings successfully and floats like a miniature yacht for a moment or two, drifting a few yards before lifting off. Trout that have up to now been feeding on rising nymphs are soon busy on the winged fly which, at this stage, is known to anglers as a dun. Its wings are of a subdued colour known to our ancestors as *dun*; in fact, the whole fly is encased in a rather opaque envelope, the last, which will presently be shed like all the others. The floating dun, or sub-imago, stage of the fly's life interests the dry-fly fisher more than any other. He exploits it most of the time he is fishing with floating imitations. Sooner or later, however, he discovers that there is another, a fourth stage of fly development, that has its own special meaning for him. This is the final metamorphosis of the typical water insect, when it discards the dun envelope and emerges as an imago or, in angler's speech, a spinner.

The dun stage is a brief enough period, useful to the angler only in its earliest moments before the fly becomes airborne. After that it usually makes for the shelter of long grasses or bushes or trees along the banks where, with little further delay, it transposes to spinner. It is now a resplendent creature, more colourful than at any previous stage, with translucent body and filmy, transparent wings. Incapable of taking food, sexually mature, it is concerned wholly with the business of propagation. Males of the various species will be seen in shimmering clouds, dancing with every appearance of the joy of life, rising and falling rhythmically in the sunshine. Their large, many-faceted, sometimes brilliant eyes are on the lookout for the more solitary females which are attracted towards the swarms. As often as one approaches, a male will detach from the rest, and copulation takes place immediately. In some species this may happen over the water. The Knotted Midge is an artificial "fly" which imitates two insects in the sexual act and on appropriate occasions can prove very successful, being much more conspicuous to trout and to angler than a single one. But usually it occurs over land, though the fertilised female makes immediately after for the water to lay her eggs. This may be done on the surface in the course of an upstream flight with frequent dippings of the abdomen in the surface tension to wash off the emerging eggs; or else the fly utilises protruding rocks or plants down which she clambers to a suitable depth. Released eggs sink to the bottom or adhere to stones or herbage where in due time they hatch and produce miniature nymphs. Throughout the egg-laying procedure the female is at the mercy of marauding trout, and when she falls spent on the surface to be carried down on the current she is eagerly sucked into the jaws of poised and expectant fish.

Meanwhile the males, who have completed their life function or are exhausted by their dance, may chance to fall back on the water. Quite a lot end up in the trout, though most of them perish over land. Spent spinners, male or female, give opportunities to the dry-fly fisher at somewhat limited times. Usually a spinner-fall takes place rather late in the day, and is a frequent cause of the famous evening rise. Male spinners often manage to survive a warm night in summer and may occasion the less well known, but very profitable, dawn rise.

The most useful group of water insects, the ephemeroptera, or day flies, have these typical four stages—egg, nymph, dun, and spinner. Other species may lack one or other stage. Stone flies have three stages—egg, creeper, and fly. The creeper is an active, legged insect which closely resembles the adult fly, lacking only the wings. Another order of water insects, the sedge or caddis flies, also have three stages—egg, larva, fly. The larval stage may be spent within a cemented case made of grains of gravel or bits of debris, or be free-swimming with shelters fixed to the under-sides of stones to which they can retreat. The caddis larva has a penultimate pupal stage not recognisable until it is extracted from its case.

Besides these flies, which all have winged forms, there are many other water creatures in the trout's larder—molluscs, shrimps, water bugs, beetles, spiders, etc, which spend their whole lives under water. Many of them are of some importance in fishing but none to the same degree as those described above.

Land-based insects which have no normal association with the water are often blown on to it and prove acceptable to the trout. Such are ants, dung flies, house flies, bluebottles, and terrestrial beetles. On my last outing of the recent season I commented to a fellow angler on the number of wasps I had seen floating down the river. I saw none taken by the trout. "They've much more sense," he replied. But trout do sometimes take bees and wasps and I doubt if they are in any danger from stings. The most successful land-based insect from the angler's point of view is the daddy-long-legs. Very wonderful imitations of it are made in Ireland, where it shares with the Mayfly the origination of a distinct form of dry-fly fishing, dapping, which is specially suited to large windy loughs where these insects are very familiar to the trout.

The life history of the typical water fly determines the three main branches of the fly-fishing art, which consists in presenting imitations of the various stages in appropriate ways so as to deceive the trout. The several vulnerable moments in the life of water insects give us three areas for presentation and thus three methods of fishing which I propose to call under-surface, on-surface, and in-surface fishing; not because I have any hope of changing the traditional terminology but in order to emphasise the special topographical characteristics of the art of fly fishing today.

PART II

Methods of Fly Fishing

[5]

Tradition and Modern Practice

*One result of the triumph of the dry fly . . . was the obliteration from
the minds of men, in much less than a generation, of all the wet fly lore
which had served many generations of chalk stream anglers well.*

G E M SKUES

Originally, as far back as Roman times and no one knows how
much farther, right up to about a century ago, there was just
fly fishing, not differentiated by name or in any other way. Then
a few technical innovations began a series of changes that were
slow to start but quickly gained momentum. The invention of
the reel and the running line ousted the loop-rod. Though the
word *cast* has been used for the action of throwing the fly by
means of the rod for a very long time, it only came to have its
modern importance when rods began to dwindle from twenty-
foot two-handers to the single-handed light wands of today. "If
you have two hands left from the Crimean or Indian Wars,"
wrote John Younger, "use both, except when you require to
scratch your lug. Thus make your angling easy, pleasurable, and
man-like." Two of these arguments are used nowadays to justify
our short rods: and itchy ears no longer trouble us.

About mid-nineteenth century, anglers on the English chalk
streams began to practise dry-fly fishing consciously and deliberately, setting in train a further series of technical developments to
make the drying and casting of the fly more successful, and some
novelties that came independently were quickly pressed into
service. Eyed hooks made replacement of flies quicker and
ensured longer lasting qualities. The study of entomology
revolutionised the traditional craft of fly tying. A theory of exact
imitation was expounded by a series of talented writers of whom
at least one was a near-genius. On the waters that suited it best,

rapidly becoming a preserve of the new rich middle class, dry fly became not just a vogue but the rule. Elsewhere more traditional methods continued, reluctantly adapting to new ideas and materials, but occasionally protesting successfully against the more bizarre and flamboyant creations of literary, deracinated anglers:

> *Awa wi your tinsey sae braw;*
> *Oor troots winna thole it ava.*
> *Wee dour looking huiks are the thing,*
> *Moose body and laverock wing.*
>
> THOMAS TOD STODDART

More recently books and magazines have markedly influenced the minds of anglers everywhere, making modern experimental methods almost universal. The latest tools and ideas became available to all and, as "progress" continues, one might expect tradition to be swamped and extinguished. If this is not happening, it is due partly to inherent conservatism and partly to the rich reservoir of ideas and practices embedded in the tradition itself. It is my strong opinion that justice has not been done to the past. In our modern hurry and conceit over our technological achievements we have denigrated and obscured our debt to the anonymous founders of the British way of angling.

G E M Skues must be given credit for beginning the rectification of the account. He is the modern inventor of nymph fishing and, being an exceptionally talented writer and lawyer, he made out a classic case for it, even for the chalk streams, sacred to the cult of the dry fly. He generously acknowledged his indebtedness to Tweed and Clydeside traditions of fly fishing and to W C Stewart, whom I describe as the heir of the folk tradition. Many a Scot when, like me, he discovered with delightful surprise Skues's gems of angling literature, *The Way of a Trout with a Fly, Chalk Stream Studies,* and *Minor Tactics,* felt like exclaiming: "We've been nymph fishing all our lives but didn't know it!" For in Scotland, after Stewart and Younger and Stoddart, the traditional methods of fishing had been reinforced at a high level of efficiency. Since their day dry-fly fishing has gradually been absorbed into this tradition (in fact, like nymph fishing, it was grafted on to roots already there) but was not allowed to distort the general pattern of practice as perhaps it did in parts of England.

Some of these assertions—the folk origin of nymph and dry fly—I have tried to prove elsewhere. There is not space in this book to develop the argument at length. I wish only to make one main point as introduction to the technical parts that follow. In the beginning, as I was saying, there was fly fishing: but it was not just *wet*-fly fishing, a term that came into use after the invention of dry-fly fishing and cast back on to the older traditional methods. It was a false cast. The older method, practised with long rod and short line, was a rich mixture. There are passages in the writings of the past that clearly show the authors were aware of the need to present a fly delicately on the surface, *without the line touching the water,* so that the fly had the optimum chance of raising a trout at the moment of impact, *before it had time to sink.* Frequent casting across or up-and-across, so as to give the shortest possible time on the water before drag set in, casting directly upstream for the same reason, insistent references to the fly *on* the water, and at least one despairing cry (by John Younger) that to make a fly capable of prolonged flotation was an impossibility—such things indicate clearly that what we call dry-fly fishing was not all that new even when it was invented but was always part of traditional practice. Given the tools of their day it is understandable that anglers felt little need to differentiate their methods. Mixed methods were very satisfactory.

Of course, they had blind spots. For instance, they would sometimes argue in favour of winged artificials even for what we would call nymph fishing. (So, too, did Skues for what he called wet-fly fishing, for the paradoxical reason that wings helped the fly to sink!) They came right to the point of discovery and recoiled. Tradition was too strong for their ideas to break through the thought barrier. Nevertheless, there is much to say in favour of their methods, more than we are sometimes willing to acknowledge, for our own practices blind us to some possibilities: for instance, that our short rods are bought at a price. We have to learn ever more complicated tricks of casting. Dare I hazard the thought that perhaps a new look at old ways may be rather overdue? But that's rather for tomorrow than for today.

[6]

Under-surface: Downstream

There is no fixed rule to be given in this question of whether to fish up or down. Every angler had better acquire both methods . . . My own experience leads me to prefer to fish across and down stream, except when the water is very small and clear in the summer. EARL GREY

Wet Fly

This is now the traditional name for the practice of fishing with a team of sunk flies. It is most appropriate on the rough river, especially in the broader and lower reaches of the larger streams. It should not be despised: in expert hands it can be very successful and is a good introductory method for beginners. In some quarters it has a bad name—"chuck-and-chance it," 'stream-raking." It does not deserve such contempt. I practise it in my later years more than ever, partly because I have taken to bigger waters and partly because I have shed some of my youthful prejudices and modified my enthusiasms for modernity.

The standard practice is to cast a fairly long line across and slightly downstream, allowing the flies to sink beneath the surface and drift down and back towards the near side as slowly as possible. The main art is this control of speed. Generally speaking, a short line increases it; a long line tends to prolong the time of the cast. The angler must study the nature of the current all the time. He may begin by fishing on his own side of the main stream first with a shortish line, perhaps even returning to the top to fish the current in the middle. If, perhaps at a third approach, he wishes to reach slacker water beyond the central current, special tactics may become necessary. When his flies alight in the slacker water beyond, the faster water in the middle will take control of the line and snatch the flies away. This snatch may excite fingerlings but seldom the larger and more cautious

trout. Two tactics are possible. Lift the rod and line, as the flies
alight, as high as possible to keep the line out of the current so
that only the leader, or little more than the leader, is in the water.
A very short rod or a wide stream makes this very difficult.
The other way is to "mend the line" as soon as it is cast, by
throwing a loop of it upstream by a sideways lift of arm and rod.
This salmon-fishing technique is quite possible with the modern
floating lines. The line will then lie on the surface in the shape
of the letter S; the time it takes for the nearer arc of the letter to
be straightened out by the speed of the faster water allows the
flies to sink in the quieter area and begin to swim downstream
at the necessary slow speed. This is the first takable moment,
immediately after the alighting of the flies. It is not dry-fly fishing,
for the flies are made to sink and travel as natural nymphs may be
expected to do, pretty nearly at the appropriate depth for mature
nymphs, that is, just under the surface.

As the stream straightens the mend and takes control of the
line the flies will be drawn across towards the middle and a lift
imparted to them at the same time. This is the second takable
moment. It is the slight acceleration and the lift that attract the
trout which has to take quickly or lose the chance.

Thereafter the flies will continue to swing round towards the
angler's bank but should be encouraged as much as possible to
drift downstream at the same time. To assist the drift and retard
the combined movement to the minimum speed the rod should
follow the line round, keeping it as straight as possible and avoiding too much belly. The arm may be extended or the angler may
even step downstream. Sometimes when fishing a slower reach
of the river the angler may practise a slow, continuous walk
downstream and reduce the number of separate casts. Otherwise,
he will usually take one or two steps between casts so that his
flies may search fresh water each time. The end of the drift is the
third takable moment; for, as the flies reach the limit of the line's
reach, they lift once more by the action of the current, and this
lift induces the take.

I have designated three takable moments in the average cast.
Of course, trout may take at any moment as long as the flies are
in the water, provided the action of the flies is near enough to
nymphal behaviour and trout are expectant. Nymphs drift more
or less at the speed of the current. They are capable of little

spurts, especially upwards, but never at a speed that creates a wake or conflicts more than momentarily with the flow of the water. That is why slow movement of the flies is so essential and drag to be avoided at all costs. Working the flies by manipulations of rod or line I find of no value at all in flowing water.

The Flies

It is usual to call any small lure made of fur, feather, silk, or materials such as these, by the name of fly. But clearly the downstream method of wet-fly fishing just described is really a form of nymph fishing. The artificials are very likely to be taken for nymphs by the trout, even when they are dressed with wings. Personally, except in loch fishing occasionally, I now never use winged artificials. Hackle flies, which are traditional in Scotland, seem to me much superior for the method, and when lightly dressed, as they should always be, very good representations of mature nymphs. Even hackle flies are not essential to the method. Purpose-made nymphs, which were originated for the upstream method, are to be recommended for downstream fishing as well. Nor is a team of nymphs or flies necessary. A single nymph fished in this way is frequently most satisfactory, and on windy days or in a bad light may avoid a lot of difficulty.

Where several flies are mounted, the tail-fly will sink deepest, though seldom more than about a foot below surface. It is good practice to position flies deliberately: for example, Goddard's P V C Nymph, which is designed to sink well, on the tail, and the famous Gold Ribbed Hare's Ear, which is thought to represent a hatching nymph, on the bob. Both represent olives. Thus the angler will be fishing at more than one level at the same time, imitating nymphs of the same species at different stages of development. This is often very satisfactory during a pronounced rise to a single identifiable species. It is also possible, of course, to fish two nymphs or wet flies of different kinds when there is doubt about the particular fly the trout are taking or when different flies are likely to be available at the same time.

The Leader

Standard practice is to have a cast or leader of several flies. Because of the ambiguity of the word "cast," the American word "leader" is coming into general use. The Clydeside "leash" would be equally good but is not likely now to catch on. Above the tail-fly are a number of droppers or short lengths of nylon, depending from the main strand at intervals, to which dropper-flies or bob-flies are attached. The top-bob, or bob-fly, may often be made to trip attractively on the surface like a dry fly or surface-trapped hatching dun, but this is possible only with a short line and practised more usually in loch fishing. Though it is sometimes advocated for the river, and has a place perhaps in late evening or night fishing with large flies, it would tend on ordinary occasions to spoil the required action of the lower flies, making them swim too fast.

The standard leader looks like this:

Fig. 2   Standard Leader

the droppers increasing slightly in length from tail to bob; though, again, this is more appropriate for loch than river fishing. The leader itself should taper, steeply from reel line towards the tail. It is usually, overall, rather less than the length of the rod, so that the union between line and leader will not foul the top ring when the line is reeled in. Some anglers like a much longer leader and attach it to the line by means of the pin knot to avoid difficulties at the top ring. The pin knot is to be recommended always, a length of nylon of about a foot or so being regarded as part of the reel line and a blood knot used for fastening on the leader itself.

The leader should taper from near line-thickness, that is, about 20 lb breaking strain, progressively to, say, 3 lb b s nylon at the tail, the strands of the taper differing by about 2 lb b s at each union. Leader knots should all be blood knots. Wherever a dropper is required the upper strand should be left protruding from the tightened knot. Flies are attached to droppers by means of the turle knot. Beware of other knots, especially "home-made" ones (though, I confess, *my* turle knot is a personal modification that has *never* failed me, which is an extraordinary claim to make). It is possible to taper the leader in its topmost section only, very steeply therefore, and to have the rest of it level, of the

D

thinnest material considered suitable. Elsewhere I discuss the question of breaking strains in more detail.

The Dropperless Leader

This innovation seems to me a great improvement on the standard one for wet-fly fishing. I first met with it on the Clyde, practised by an angler who went in for upwards of a dozen flies to his leash. Some time afterwards I experimented quite a lot and adapted it to my own use, discovering in the process what I consider are its special advantages. I had been using it for at least ten years before I came across an early description of it in print, in Stoddart's *The Angler's Companion*, second edition, dated 1853. Here is the reference:

"In a small publication upon fly-fishing, by Captain Clarke, RN, a new method of making up the fly-cast is introduced under the name of the rapid-stream tackle. It consists simply of dressing the upper flies over the joinings of the different lengths of gut, instead of appending them at fixed intervals as droppers— consequently they will be ranged along the lower casting or foot line at a distance from each other averaging fifteen inches; and should the above mentioned portion of the throwing tackle measure ten feet, they will mount in number, inclusive of the trail-hook, to seven or eight. This tackle the author of the treatise in question recommends as highly serviceable when employed on rapid streams or under a strong wind; and he mentions having accomplished a feat with it in the neighbourhood of Coldstream which is certainly without precedent in the annals of trout fishing."

Fortunately, perhaps, I worked on this idea before reading the above, so that I was able to have different objectives. I don't advocate a multiplicity of flies at very short intervals. Usually two flies suffice and never more than three. The first advantage I saw in it was simplicity of construction and alteration. The second which impressed itself on me in the course of trial, was the behaviour of the flies, satisfying the important criterion o liveliness. Here is the dropperless-leader:

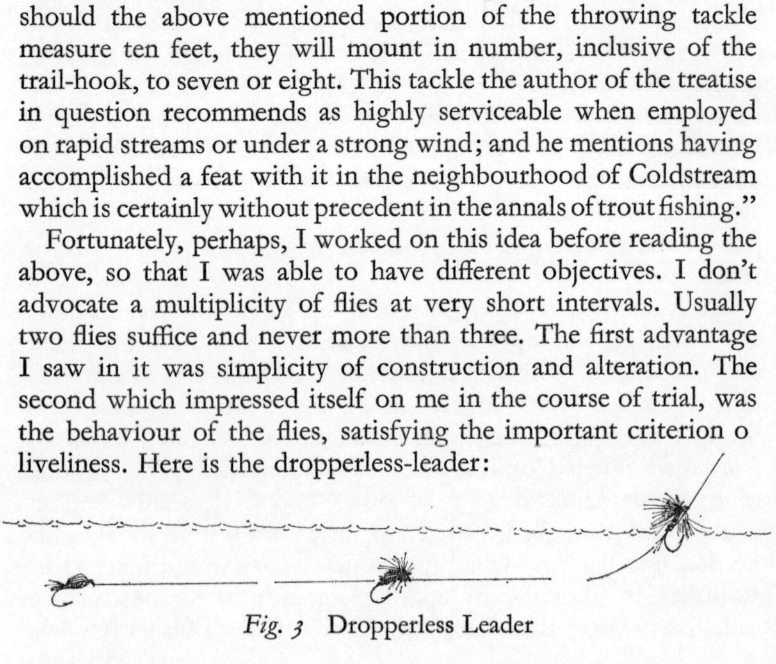

Fig. 3 Dropperless Leader

All flies, except the tail, are simply threaded through the eye on to the main links. They are not tied in any way: the links are knotted below each fly, so that the flies abut against the knots. Thus the upper flies are free to move, to oscillate, in response to water movement and must for that reason appear very lively. There are no dropper lengths, which, on the standard leader, add to the foreign material in the neighbourhood of each fly: thus the new one is much less cluttersome than the old. The real test, of course, is how it operates in action. After some twenty years' regular practice with it I have not the slightest inclination to go back to the older form. I cannot claim feats "without precedent in the annals of trout fishing", nor even to be more than moderately expert in the art which I practise for pleasure, but I catch as many trout as the other fellow and no less than I did before I changed my end tackle. I can invent as many theoretical objections to it as anyone else (I did so in my earlier experimenting) but they just don't affect the main issue, that the dropperless leader is better by reason of its simplicity and, in my experience, also more successful. I use it for the rough stream undersurface method, for ordinary loch fishing, for the occasional times when I mount two dry flies, or nymph with dry-fly indicator: in fact, whenever I have need of more than one artificial at a time.

Signs of the Take

During the fishing out of a cast the line may be held against the rod handle by the forefinger of the casting hand. If the line and leader are not slack in the water the slightest touch on a fly will be felt. Often a trout will hook itself: but a break is always possible, especially if a big fish takes in a heavy stream. I prefer holding the line in the inner groove of the top joint of the forefinger, so that it is free to run, even when the grip tightens, while the finger applies a gentle brake. Thus the strike is partly against the finger, partly from the reel.

Many takes will register by touch, but visual indications should always be looked for and are usually better and always more exciting. I use a white line nowadays which is easily kept in view, and I try to watch it, or the area in which the flies are operating, or both. A take deep down will signal itself by a sharp draw of the line or straightening of the curve. This will usually precede the tangible signal. Surface indications in the neighbourhood of the flies will range from none at all to a porpoise roll which reveals the whole fish. In clear water with a penetrating light the gleam of a turning fish will sometimes show. Experience will perhaps provide an angler, who has learned to concentrate, with an uncanny skill in detecting the slightest alteration in the surface patterns. He will react to intimations others might never see and indeed ones that leave no conscious trace in his own mind. This is not really magic but sheer skill. At all signals the rod should be smartly raised from the fishing position, which should never be less than about 30° with the surface, so that there is no delay in tightening on the fish. A lot of slack, or a horizontal rod, is a serious handicap: in either case the rod has to move a considerable distance before it has any effect. A tight line from a horizontal rod puts all the strain on the fine end of the leader, without any benefit from the spring of the rod, and often results in a broken point, when a heavy trout takes confidently, or in the tearing out of a lightly engaged hook. The recommended fishing angle makes sure the rod's spring is immediately brought into action.

Miss-takes

A common criticism of the under-surface method is the number of missed strikes, frequent plucks at the flies with no other result. This is the case when small fish bother the angler or when the flies are being fished incorrectly; but it may sometimes happen in seemingly excellent circumstances. A change of fly, hook size, or length of line, may make a difference. When fish are really on the feed the proportion of takes to offers is usually much higher. There is validity in the criticism, though other methods are not necessarily so much better. Favourable conditions tend to favour all methods.

Landing a Trout

By the downstream method a hooked trout may have to be played below the angler. If it chooses to come upstream it should be encouraged to do so, always on a firm line. If it is in, or gets into, a heavy stream and goes down, it should be allowed to draw line with the rod held high. "Give it the butt" is a dangerous exaggeration of this advice. The principle to keep in mind is: a tight line and a flexed rod, but not flexed to its full extent, so that it can still give to a sudden plunge without too much strain on the leader or hook hold. As soon as possible the fish should be guided towards the side and slacker water, where, whenever it gives an opportunity, it may be brought up towards the angler. It usually obliges in slack water. Beware of shortening line too soon with a big fish that still has a lot of fight. It should be allowed several rushes within the quieter area of water to expend some of its energy. Too short a line too soon often results in violent splashing on the surface. This may itself be the result of a weak hold, instinctively appreciated by the fish: it often causes even a good hold to weaken and the loss of the fish. Slightly lower the rod and the trout will get below the surface again. As soon as possible complete the fight, but not until you can get the fish's head above surface, when it usually gives in. Sink the net in the water and draw the trout over the rim; then lift both with a firm movement. Never try to scoop a fish which is below the surface. Netting technique will be varied by the angler when he has gained experience. Small fish may often be bustled unceremoniously, but not violently, into the net; or brought to hand and lifted out of the water. Always wet the hand, if a fish is to be returned, so as not to remove the protective slime from the scales, which may expose the fish to ever-present spores of fungoid disease or interfere with the osmotic system that controls the salinity of its body tissues.

[7]

Under-surface: Upstream

*Nymph fishing . . . is a very exacting form of fly-fishing, infinitely more
exacting than the dry-fly.*   OLIVER KITE

I cannot explain just what method is mine,
But experience, when you have bought her,
Will tighten your line
At a hint of a sign
Of a ghost of a wink under water.

G E M SKUES

This difficult form of fly fishing humbles experts and challenges
the ambitious. Modest performers in other methods admire it
and suffer agonising crises of confidence in their efforts to learn
it, which is my own case. Nevertheless, I keep practising both it
and philosophy, greatly hopeful, only moderately successful.
Time's thievish progress threatens even my hopes. I recommend
it to my fellow anglers and wish them better satisfactions.

It is at once a classic and contemporary method. It was advocated long ago by my favourite Scottish triumvirate, Younger,
Stoddart, and Stewart. The last insisted on it for the smaller
rough streams and devised his own "spiders" for the job. Early
this century Skues rediscovered it, named it nymph fishing, and,
by force of charm, logic, and intellect restored it to the streams
of the south in spite of considerable opposition. Frank Sawyer
and Oliver Kite, by example, book, and broadcast, have made it a
contemporary challenge to fly fishers everywhere. It is still in
its modern formative period and inspires much experimentation
especially with modern materials such as gantron and p v c.

When I read of Sawyer using it instead of net or electric
stunning to remove scores of unwanted grayling from his stream,
or of Oliver Kite watching his trout's mouth whiten at the take

which he has "induced" with a "bare" hook—when I read these wonders, I'm apt to think it belongs really to the crystal chalk streams and not to the waters I mostly fish, where trout are hard to see and presumably easier to catch by other methods; until I remember Stewart's amused exasperation with the incorrigibles he used to meet on the river, still fishing downstream with copies of his *Practical Angler* in their pockets, complaining of lack of sport. Of course, it belongs to the rough stream also. It's me that's wrong.

If, in what follows, a hint of irony is detectable in my description of upstream nymph fishing, put it down to envy; envy not for the other man's opportunities but rather for his skill. "I envy nobody but him," Walton ingenuously confessed, "and him only, that catches more fish than I do." I'm less interested in numbers of fish, though they measure what I envy more, namely, the expertise of the angling virtuoso. Upstream nymph fishing today is the method that reveals him.

Technique

It resembles dry-fly fishing in many respects. A single fly or nymph is mounted at the end of a tapered leader with a long last link of the thinnest practicable nylon. This is pitched, rather than cast up the water, so that the nylon point curves downwards and the nymph goes under at once, along with a foot or so of leader. It swims down at the speed of the current and at a required depth, either just under the surface or farther below it, according to where the trout are finding their food at the time. The angler maintains a taut line for instant readiness.

He fishes the water, the rise, or the trout itself. On the rough stream, where many more trout may be on the feed than show at the surface and where trout beneath are not easily seen, the nymph will be sent out to fish every likely lie. Casts may be in any more or less upward direction; and across-stream casting, which is a favourable tactic, makes this method approximate to that described in the previous chapter. The angler must acquire an eye for water so as to recognise by surface pattern in the current all the sorts of places where trout may be expected to lurk. The sides of strong streams, the neighbourhood of rocks, undercut banks, deeper channels in shallow rushes, smooth patches below, or in the midst of, broken water, the spread of the pool where the entering stream smoothes out, the glass edge or cushion of calm under a lee bank—experience teaches the rough-stream angler to recognise these and other favourable locations where trout are likely to be lying in wait for the living drift. On small clear waters which have low unencumbered banks he will make his approaches from the land using every artifice of cunning to avoid detection by the trout. But on wider rivers much of the water would be unapproachable if he did not meet the fish in their own element. There are serious considerations to beware of when wading but also real advantages. One of these is that the angler is always low on the trout's horizon and is able to get closer to it without scare: and shorter casts improve his control of line and nymph.

The Induced Take

Fish, even when feeding on nymphs, often break surface, usually at the turn. These are not true rises but help the beginner to recognise typical lies. Any such rise should be covered if it is within reach. It should be noted, however, that the action of the current often shows the movement of a trout considerably below its true position, and the deeper the fish when it turns, the farther downstream the surface indication. The artificial may be dropped above a marked spot and a voluntary take expected. If nothing happens, another cast may be made above and slightly to the near side of the lie. As the nymph swims into the trout's vicinity, a lift may be given to it. This is the tactic of the "induced take". It attracts trout to an apparently live morsel of food and may persuade it to turn aside for it. It often does so quite savagely and hooks itself on the return. On very favourable days, when surface indications are frequent, the angler may proceed quickly from rise to rise, ignoring other areas. Trout rising to surface fly, especially in shallow water, are not likely to ignore a nymph just because it is slightly under water: they are often feeding on nymphs and duns simultaneously. As a rule, however, the rough stream encourages fishing the water. A constant look out for fish breaking or humping the surface and careful attention to such opportunities increase interest and success.

Strict chalk stream practice is to survey the pool and discover feeding fish which then become marked targets. In these circumstances the special skills of the method really come into their own.

There is no hurry. The angler watches his intended victim to discover how and at what depth it is feeding and to take account of anything that may help or hinder his presentation of the fly. He proceeds only when he has worked out a suitable mode of attack. Experience and familiarity with the water will make this preliminary assessment brief as well as accurate. Then he offers the nymph to the chosen fish, wherever possible the largest within range; or else the smaller fish that intervene between him and his main prize are expeditiously taken out one after another until only the monarch of the pool remains. A perfect cast puts the nymph on track, beyond and to the near side. It sinks at once and drifts within reach of the trout. As it passes, an irresistible urge to seize it is induced in the trout by a delicate lift of rod and line. The nymph rises, the trout turns, the mouth whitens, the angler strikes, and the fight is on.

To observe the turn and actual take, or even only the "little brown wink underwater" that Skues taught us to look for as the sign of it, is only possible in very clear calm water, at near distance, and in direct light. More often these circumstances are not available. The water is drumly, the surface rippled or silvered with reflected light. The upstream fisher is denied the down-streamer's expectation of a tug on the line when other signals fail. Trout are extraordinarily quick to eject a mistaken mouthful. They do so without panic, as a matter of cautious habit, just as they eject other harmless samples of drift. It is only too easy to notice nothing and to proceed with the fishing ever more despairingly, quite unaware of the nymph's success in *attracting* the trout. It's the angler who must *hook* it by a skill that requires constant alertness to minimum indications. Instead of complaining—

> *I'd like you to tell*
> *How the (qualified) hell*
> *I'm to know I've a wink underwater*

—look for alternative signs.

The first requirement is a good floating line, one that is easily seen on the water and of lighter weight than is usually recommended for dry fly, so as to be sensitive to slight pulls by the trout. The leader's dipping point, however, is a more reliable guide to action than the line itself. Many nymph fishers heavily grease the leader to within a foot or so of the hook and use mud or glycerine to make sure the final stretch sinks readily. They watch the little hole in the surface through which the end of the leader disappears. This is where, in Oliver Kite's vivid simile, "you may expect to see the sinking cast accelerate slightly in the event of a fish taking your nymph, rather like the sally part of a belfry upper floor through which the bell-rope descends sharply as the ringer on the floor below pulls on the bell-rope sally". Another means of detecting takes is to mount a dry fly about two feet above the nymph. When the latter is taken the tell-tale skids across the surface or is drawn under: and there is always the possibility of a bonus trout on the dry fly itself.

The Nymphs

The influence of dry-fly tradition gave some of the earlier nymph fishers a lot of trouble. They had difficulty in getting their nymphs to sink promptly and seemed to have scruples about obvious means. They discarded waterproof materials, such as quill for bodies, and experimented with absorbent dubbings. Skues even recommended the retention of wings because they retained moisture and so helped the fly to sink; but he soon passed that stage and designed true nymphal representations that were models of fly-tying craft and have been imitated by many followers. Hackles, to represent legs or gills of the natural nymph, have dwindled to the merest wisps or have been altogether discarded. It is only quite recently, however, that the use of lead or copper wire to add weight has triumphed over purist scruples. On some waters wired nymphs are disallowed, though becoming acceptable generally. There's no reason, of course, why a fishery should not make its own rules, such as dry fly only, or dry fly and unweighted nymph, or any other variation of practice it likes. Fly fishing is a sophisticated sport. There are simpler methods of taking fish: anglers will always have to determine just where they wish to draw the line!

It is natural to expect a variety of patterns to be recommended, representing the several species of insects to be found in any water at a given season. March Brown, Spring Olive, Iron Blue nymph tyings are described in many books. I, too, have been interested in a variety, derived from such flies as I normally use when dry-fly fishing. I long hesitated to believe in too much simplification. In recent years I have modified my opinions considerably. Still rather amazed at its success, I have found a single pattern, in varying sizes, quite adequate, namely Sawyer's Pheasant Tail nymph tied with copper wire. It represents nymphs of the olive tribe and there are usually plenty of them in the water at taking times to provide for reasonable sport. But I don't yet fish exclusively with it. I have one or two recipes of my own, a Greenwell derivation, for instance; but I see no good reason to force it on the attention of the public in competition with others. I would be very reluctant to abandon that ancient stand-by, the Gold Ribbed Hair Lug. Nevertheless, in this most difficult of all branches of fly fishing, here is a surprising aspect of simplicity which should appeal to beginners and help to start them on a practice which will surely lead to mastery if they persist during early difficulties and inevitable frustrations. Later on they may like to carry a more varied selection such as is recommended in a later chapter dealing with the selection of artificial flies.

[8]

On-surface: Dry Fly

Those who know and practise the art best are the epicures amongst anglers; they have carried both the skill and pleasure of angling to a height of exquisite refinement.　　　　　　　　EARL GREY

A French book I was reading not long ago described dry-fly fishing as an elegant sport, basically easy to learn, but complained of "tout d'abord, une grosse part de snobisme dans la pratique. ... Les 'snobs' la compliquèrent". I would have thought this was no longer true. An altogether healthier ideal of it, as one fascinating branch of angling among others, has succeeded the puristic nonsense that affected discussion for so long.

Perhaps the sport would have taken a better course earlier if it had begun in France—or in Scotland, as it well might have done. I have a regret that my hero, Stewart, the practical angler himself, was unable to transcend the limitations of his very qualities. He is a paradox. By his practice he set Scots nymph fishing, in all but name, half a century before Skues; whereas his theory—he was always averse to theory—tended straight towards dry fly but hesitated at the critical point. "After your flies alight, allow them to float gently down stream for a yard or two, taking care that neither they nor the line ripple the surface": this is pure dry-fly instruction. Then, instead of affirming what, in 1857, would have been a new and revolutionary principle, he had a tragic failure of inspiration and concluded with a negative reiteration of conventional technique: "There is no occasion for keeping them on the surface; they will be just as attractive a few inches under water."

To do just what Stewart discounted, to keep them always on the surface, is the essence of the dry-fly art and constitutes it as a distinct branch of angling. There is plenty of occasion for it on all kinds of water, whether rough stream or chalk. It is a superficial art. Its discovery (as distinct from its subsequent development) should have been possible as a result of easy observation of surface incidents, whereas nymph fishing depends on fairly accurate knowledge of underwater phenomena. Yet its discovery was surprisingly retarded.

Not Difficult

I now hesitate to call it easy, though that's really what I believe. I was asked to advise a beginner. Why shouldn't he start, I reasoned, with the two-dimensional art of dry fly and leave the three-dimensional wet fly till later? That will get rid of his inferiority complex: for he had already expressed the common opinion about the exceptional difficulty of dry fly and the rare qualities it demands.

So I tried to get him to cast a floating fly upstream. He couldn't. A gentle downstream breeze defeated his attempts; no trout would look at his fly in the coil of nylon he surrounded it with. When I met him again an hour later he was facing the other way, rejoicing at the plucks he was having from salmon parr. Before the day's end he took one of them home to prove his prowess!

Easy, superficial, two-dimensional. . . .

It's really five-dimensional, two on the water and three in the air. Wet fly is six-dimensional, three in the water and three, easier ones, in the air. A beginner is likely to be persuaded by the aerial aspects. His failures there are obvious and frustrating; in upstream casting the current doesn't rectify his casting errors.

Nevertheless, I regret the inhibiting myth that dry fly is beyond the skill of ordinary anglers. On the contrary, it is capable of giving delight to anyone with a modicum of determination, however modest his skill or experience. Pleasure aids skill; and dry-fly fishing has its special pleasures. It concentrates attention on the top of the water, that magic looking-glass through which trout and man mysteriously make acquaintance with each other. Their confrontation is a series of sudden excitements. Its practice alone, the casting and presentation of the fly, is almost a sport in itself, giving aesthetic satisfactions almost without the bonus of fish.

In the rest of this chapter I deal with its special characteristics and problems in more detail—all except the most important of all, choice of fly, which is reserved for fuller treatment separately.

Times for Dry Fly

A common error, if catching trout is the objective, is to fish dry fly when the occasion is unsuitable. Time rather than place is the criterion here. One may fish on the surface almost anywhere. There are few impossible places, unless those out of reach, even on the roughest streams. The light-hearted pirouette of a dry fly, elegantly poised on its shining hackle points, as it dances down a stickle or a cataract, is as lovely to watch as its statelier progress on the even surface of a pool. In such places the trout are often quite eager to join the dance.

To continue on-surface fishing when the trout have withdrawn their attention is not reasonable. There are many times when under-surface fishing is better. During the early weeks of the season dry fly will pay off for relatively short periods of most days, and even then the trout may be, as Stewart said, just as pleased with flies travelling an inch or two under the surface, being eager enough for food at any level. By May, and through to mid-June, dry fly will have come into its own, possible or even necessary from morning to dusk. Thereafter, throughout the dog-days, which are the despair of beginners and holiday anglers, until August is almost gone, nymph fishing is likely to be much more successful, though demanding skill of a high order. The last few weeks of the season, like spring, will again give opportunities for both methods, with the balance of advantage still to nymph. The vagaries of wind and weather complicate deductions from the calendar alone. It is always a matter of observation. The angler who has, or seeks to have, both skills will change from one to other according to surface indications. He will learn to discriminate (though the difference is not all that critical) between rises proper, when trout are taking duns or spinners on the surface, and the effects of "bulging" trout working just below it. Because of its special delights he may prefer to switch to dry fly whenever he gets the chance. Over the season, on the rough stream, nymph fishing in one form or other is likely to prove more rewarding in terms of catch; whereas on the chalk streams dry fly and nymph are comparatively well-matched competitors, though affected by some weather and seasonal variation.

On-surface fly fishing exploits a very short period in the life history of some of the aquatic insects that contribute to the trout's food supply—namely the dun and spinner stages, and these only when they are on the water, which is a further limitation of time. The fisherman who elects to fish dry fly only is condemning himself to long periods of inactivity or else to a form of activity that deserves the name of art for art's sake. The probability of finding an occasional trout ready to take an artificial dry fly in the absence of natural flies is higher on some waters than on others, and these odd fish may satisfy some anglers who prefer to specialise; but most of us look for more constant rewards; which is why under-surface fly fishing persisted, or made a come-back, on most of our waters.

Advantages of the Method

The upstream method, for either nymph or dry fly, can claim special advantages. Because the approach is from a downstream position, in rear of the fish, there is greater chance of escaping notice. If the angle of attack is to either side of it, this advantage, theoretically, is lost since it depends on a rear blind angle of some 30°. In practice, however, as experience shows, the advantage is a real one and extends beyond the limit of the fish's blind region. It is quite surprising how near one may approach a feeding trout without alarming it if necessary precautions are taken. The explanation may have to do with attention. The trout's interest is directed mainly forwards, or forwards and sideways, as it is looking for food borne down by the current. We tend not to see what we are not interested in: we switch our attention away from it. I feel sure trout behave similarly and thus give us our opportunities. They don't see what they are not attending to. They are, however, timid creatures, capable of seeing all around them. If anything arouses their apprehension, they will immediately attend to it. Moreover, a very slight head movement will even abolish the blind rear angle. The fisherman, therefore, must approach his quarry with the utmost caution so as not to attract attention. This is, fortunately, very possible, much more so than might have been expected. He must keep low and thus below, or only on the edge of, the horizon of the trout's window. Wading helps in this. When casting from the bank every form of cover, behind or in front of the angler, should be utilised, or he should kneel on the bank. In general and in addition to these precautions, he can depend on the trout's blind area and the still more extensive area of its inattention, if he has the skill and self-control to do so. A thorough understanding of these conditions helps in practice. I shall have occasion later to discuss these problems in another connection.

The approach, therefore, need not be directly upstream. Experienced dry-fly men fish in almost any direction. Across stream is sometimes more profitable than any other; and downstream casting has its special occasions as well as its special difficulties. Carefulness of approach is a paramount requirement.

Two other advantages result from upstream casting. It is a majority opinion that trout are more easily hooked when the strike is a downstream pull; and fewer trout are pricked as they take and eject the fly. A minority argument is that, at the moment of taking, the trout may not be facing upstream, having turned to take the fly; or else, because the cast was not directly upstream the strike may not be a downstream one. In either case the advantage is lost or reduced. There's something in this argument, but it does not really invalidate the other. By the law of economy of effort, a trout merely tilts upwards and sucks in a fly as it floats towards its neb and this, therefore, is the norm. Even on the fewer occasions when a trout swings out of its lie, takes the fly and immediately returns, even if the strike is not mainly downstream, as often as not it is in a direction almost opposite to the returning movement of the trout. A *sideways* pull at the strike is, therefore, not much inferior to a downstream one and surely much better than an upstream pull, which tends just to withdraw the hook either before the trout has closed its mouth or as it opens it again to eject the inedible item. Upstream fishing, therefore, with directional variations, is undoubtedly more efficient in lodging the hook.

The second advantage is uncontested. The fly is presented on water undisturbed by the act of fishing. A hooked fish is played to the net below the position of hooking. In fact, after a day or two's intensive dry-fly fishing on holiday the whole process of casting, watching the downward drift of the floating fly, seeing the rise of a trout, striking, and tumbling a fish rapidly down and into the opened net—all this tends to become almost automatic: so much so that sometimes I have a fish in the net and have no awareness of these stages of action. Unconscious fishing of this kind might seem the opposite of enjoyment. Not so, the whole procedure is such an exercise of skill that the overall feeling is one of intense pleasure. One's whole being seems in perfect co-ordination. After each fish is taken, casting may recommence immediately, except when the fisherman's activity in playing and netting, perhaps, a larger than usual fish in very calm water may have alerted the attention of trout in the immediate neighbourhood; in such case it may be wise to rest the pool for a few moments before carrying on.

Presenting the Fly

Normally one fly is presented. There are exceptions to this rule. If the end fly is difficult to see in the conditions of light or water, a more conspicuous one may be mounted as a dropper. By means of such a guide, rises to the inconspicuous fly are less likely to be missed. It sometimes pays to put on a general fly above a specific one. The former may take an occasional trout in addition to the selective feeders who may go for the latter, if it is the right pattern. If, as often is the case, the specific fly is wrongly diagnosed, some success is thus likely during the period of trial and error to find the right specific pattern. Two different flies of likely patterns, when it is not certain what the trout are after, may be used exploratively. After the raising or catching of a fish on one of them the unsuccessful fly may be removed altogether or replaced with another of the successful pattern: during a boiling rise two flies of the right sort may increase the number of offers.

A dry-fly dropper may be used as indicator when a nymph is being fished on the tail; or these positions may be reversed. The dry fly will dart across or under water when the nymph is taken and, in some circumstances or for some fishers, may be a better sign than the draw of the dipping point of the leader. If the indicator and the nymph are representations of the same insect at two stages of development, there is a good chance of takes at both since trout are not always selective in this respect.

Thus, two flies are sometimes useful, though the rule of a single fly is not invalidated by these exceptions. A single is easier

E

to present; and presentation is the secret of dry-fly fishing. A second fly catches the wind and causes misplacement of both; for the same reason it limits length of cast; and although one or other of two flies will be easier to detect on the water, the chances of missing rises, in spite of what was said above, instead of being reduced are actually sometimes increased. A single fly should be regarded as the norm, since it is more likely to assist accuracy at every stage from cast to strike.

Flotation

The fly must float well. Therefore it is made of non-absorbent materials or such as readily discard moisture. Hackles, to represent legs of an insect, must be stiff and sharp. Cock hackles satisfy this requirement, hen hackles being more useful for sinking flies. An insect has only six legs. The trout can't count but it learns to recognise the impress pattern on the surface skin of the water made by the feet of a floating fly: this pattern means food to it. An artificial should convey the same meaning. A bottle brush may or may not succed, but never because it resembles a delicate day fly in dun or spinner stage. An artificial should have as many points as are necessary to make it float—certainly therefore more than six in number—anything bushier may fail to deceive the trout, especially if it is feeding selectively. First-class hackles, sparingly dressed, are much superior to poor ones crowded on the hook.

Some Necessary Equipment

A fully equipped dry-fly fisher is an excellent subject of caricature. Two items, mysterious to non-fishers, are the little bottle of oil dangling from a jacket button and beside it a tiny plastic wallet of amadou. Even the name of amadou is a subject of mirth. Chemists nowadays seem to have forgotten its value as a stauncher of bleeding and no longer stock it. If you ask them for amadou a strange look appears in their eyes and presently a pitying sort of smile. I think they only hear the second syllable and feel sorry for you. Any attempt to explain that amadou is a sort of dried fungus only makes things worse. Therefore, get your small supply from a fishing-tackle dealer (most now stock it) or use paper tissue or even your handkerchief instead. Unfortunately, wet hands spoil the paper or the handkerchief for this job, and amadou remains the best; a very valuable accessory. A water-logged fly pressed between two layers of amadou immediately loses all its moisture and is ready for oiling.

For years I was quite content with medicinal paraffin but nowadays, I suppose, silicone fly float is better. After using amadou to remove water, the fly should be lightly touched with an oiled feather or brush, or sprayed from a pressurised can. Any surplus oil can be removed by blowing on the fly or by means of a false cast. I have been told that the French, who seem rapidly to be taking the lead in trout fishing practice, now have a means of waterproofing flies, once and for all, in the making. Whether that would eliminate the need for false casting to expel water from a drowned fly, I don't know. At present every time a fly is lifted from the water it is usual to aerialise it by one or two false casts in which extra force is applied to the back and forward drives: this whisks off moisture clinging to the hackle or body material. Two tests of a good fisher might be: his sparing use of false casting, which in excess increases fatigue, and his care to make false casts in a different direction from the final one so as not to alert the trout. False casting is also a method of measuring the length of line extended to reach the trout's position, extra line being pulled out from the reel by means of the left hand between each cast until the necessary length is out.

Gentle Alightment

The fly must alight gently so as not to break through the surface or alarm the fish. This thistledown doctrine was taught and practised long before dry fly was recognised by name. It is necessary when a marked fish is aimed at, since to alert it is to lose it. A fly that splashes down and continues to float may, of course, succeed in taking a fish some distance below its point of alighting. Violent presentations are not always wasted. Sometimes there is no alternative to slamming the fly down on the water, as for instance, when the cast has to be made in the teeth of a wind. Delicate presentation, however, is generally very important. To achieve it the cast should be aimed not at a spot *on* the water but a foot or so *above* the water, so that, when the force of the cast has expended itself, the fly may be allowed to fall gently to the surface, parachuted by its hackle. This is not usually such a very difficult art: flies with horizontal "parachute"-type hackles have been designed specially to meet this requirement but, though good, these are not really necessary. Most presentations should be made to a spot above the trout's lie to avoid any disturbance frightening it and to give the fish time to see it approaching as it crosses its window. Sometimes, after a refusal, the fly may be made to fall right over the trout's nose, which gives it little time for consideration and may result in a rise by reflex action. By nature a trout is a snapper up of unconsidered trifles in case they escape. It is equally fast in ejecting anything inedible and nothing else is so dangerous as a hook.

The Strike

When a dry fly is taken there is usually a clear surface indication: sometimes, indeed, the trout displays its whole form as it breaks through the surface and returns with the fly in its mouth. This exciting occurrence illustrates the principle of the dry-fly strike. It should be made as the fish turns down with the fly, not before, and not delayed too long or the hook will have been ejected. Trout have large mouths and easily expel unwanted materials. Even when little else is seen but the disappearance of the fly in the centre of a surface ring, which is quickly obliterated by the current, it may be assumed that the trout has turned down. The strike is made, therefore, after a slight pause to allow for the turn and thereby operates against the weight of the fish which causes the hook to bite. When it is accurately timed the danger is of breaking the nylon point. This happens when the strike is too violent or the fish heavier than expected, which comes to the same thing. As explained previously, I advocate a gently-braked line rather than a tightly-held one, which reduces the risk of broken points but provides enough resistance to lodge the hook. Timing and controlling the strike go together. Excitement may spoil both actions. Dry-fly fishing is exciting: the fisherman has to enjoy his excitements in a deliberate sort of way; otherwise he'll get plenty of thrills and few fish, which spells exasperation.

Timing is a matter of experience. More often than not the fisherman is too quck, but ascribes his fault to the virtue of the trout. He tries to increase his speed of reaction and makes things worse. Wet-fly fishing, which demands instant responses, has perhaps conditioned his hand and eye. He has to unlearn part of his training: but once the dry-fly knack has been acquired it is seldom lost, and switching from one skill to another becomes much easier. Nevertheless, fishing is a complex art, thank goodness; there are many variables which defeat rules of thumb. One of these is size of trout. In dry-fly fishing a slower strike is appropriate for a larger trout, especially when it has shown itself. A dimple or a bulge on the surface requires a very short pause before striking, as the turn has probably been completed before the angler has seen the indication. In any consistent circumstances some experiment at successive rises between long and short pauses, slow and fast striking, may be made to determine the more successful. If paused striking fails, the strike should be speeded up. Begin with the pause.

Avoidance of Drag

Casting, presentation, striking—these three skills are essential for successful dry-fly fishing. A fourth must now be added. Perhaps it is the most difficult of all: skill can minimise the problem involved but cannot eliminate it. It is the problem of drag. If the fly hook were not attached to a line it would float on the surface at the pleasure of the current as naturally as the real insect: but the fly is tethered and the line may stretch across water flowing at different speeds in different parts. The current pulls on the line and the fly is dragged off course and made to riffle the surface. This unnatural behaviour is usually fatal to success. Very occasionally at the beginning of the drag a fish will be stimulated to have a go: but a rare occurrence such as this doesn't contradict the rule that drag is bad. It may be avoided by direct upstream casting which puts fly and line in the same strand of the current and the fly maintains a natural course. A disadvantage of direct upstream casting is that a fish may be "lined", that is, covered by the line before the fly appears. Although lining a fish does not put a fish down in every instance, careful dry-fly fishers often prefer a more oblique cast at the risk of drag: the more oblique and the longer the cast the greater the likelihood. Avoidance or limitation of drag is a constant problem. It is good practice, after you have successfully learned how to cast a straight line, to learn how to make a wriggly cast. Extra force in the forward drive is one method; this causes the line to halt with a jerk and telescope backwards (it is hoped); more often, only the fly springs back and lies beside the line on the water. A better method is to wiggle the rod top at the conclusion of the drive, so as to put a curve, or, better still, a number of small curves on the water to give the current some line to work on before its action affects the drift of the fly. Always, when the cast has been more or less across stream, the drift of the line should be followed by the rod, in an effort to prevent a belly developing: a belly quickly drags a fly off course. Mending line may occasionally be possible when fishing across. The fly will almost certainly receive a sharp momentary drag by the act of mending, but this may be preferable to a prolonged riffling of the surface which a bellied line is likely to cause. The wriggly cast remains, however, the best treatment for drag, assisted by frequent casting to anticipate its onset. Frequent casting, in any case, is a feature of dry-fly fishing, because the current is always bringing the fly back from above. It is a very active, sometimes exhausting, mode of catching trout.

The full enjoyment of dry-fly fishing is experienced on a day of frequent rises. These may be sporadic throughout the day, or concentrated into longer or shorter periods at intervals. When fish are rising in a steady fashion, the angler may cast his flies carefully over rise forms in confident expectation of responses. He may know the fly on the water by distant observation and acquired experience, or he may have caught up a specimen and chosen a suitable representation. On many such days the trout will not be too choosy, and from time to time one will rise to a well-placed artificial. Though tingling with delight the angler will control his nerves, strike judiciously, feel the plunge of a hooked fish, and hear his reel sing. His rod will have been held well above the horizontal and now is lifted higher, so that it arcs to the pull of the trout, insures against breakage, and performs as an instrument of pleasure in his hand. Every moment of dry-fly fishing, from presentation of fly to netting of fish, is a sheer and agonising delight; approached but, in my opinion, not excelled by any other method.

[9]

In-surface:
Stuck Nymph and Spinner-fall

A particularly dangerous period in the life of an ephemeropteran is that immediately before, during, and immediately after the emergence of the dun from the nymphal shuck.   J R HARRIS

Under-surface and on-surface fishing are now clearly defined methods by whatever name they are known. Both are practicable for long enough periods of most days to enable an angler to specialise, if he so wishes. In-surface fishing is not likely to achieve this status. Though it has a clearly defined area, it is not appropriate often enough or long enough to encourage specialism. It is not, in fact, a single method but rather a variety, related to both nymph and dry fly. Its occasions are sometimes hard to recognise and its means difficult to determine. By the time the right fly has been chosen the opportunity may have passed. It is, however, a challenge to understanding; and, as a fisherman gathers experience, he may come to value challenges more highly than fish. In-surface fishing is a test of observation, understanding, and skill.

There are three main occasions for it on the river:

(*a*) when rising nymphs are struggling through the surface film;

(*b*) when the nymph, or even the hatched dun, gets stuck in the film;

(*c*) at spinner-fall.

The still-water fisherman has an occasion of his own somewhat similar to (*a*) and (*b*) above, namely:

(*d*) when midge-pupae are floating, as they do naturally, in the surface film.

The first of these, the rising of mature nymphs, is a time of high drama, exciting to the trout and, therefore, fraught with peril for the flies, which are more exposed than at any previous time of their lives. Skues's artificial nymphs were the first deliberate attempt to exploit this occasion. They represented mature larvae with conspicuous wing buds approaching the undersurface. Sawyer's wired artificials exploit earlier stages of nymphal development. Between them these men have established undersurface nymph fishing as we know it today, in two varieties of one distinctive method.

Skues was well aware that nymphs, having reached the surface, often get stuck in the tension. I think he was inclined to regard this as a special case of dry-fly fishing. He describes an incident when his fly was repeatedly refused until it became waterlogged, when the trout immediately accepted it; after that he was able to take some other fish with half-drowned dry flies. Many other anglers have had this experience and have recommended removing oil and reducing the dressing of orthodox floating flies as *ad hoc* tactics. Today in-surface fishing in its own right is being given a great deal of attention by expert and knowledgeable fly tyers. John Goddard and his friend, Cliff Henry, are designing purpose-made artificials, notably their Hatching Nymph, to deceive trout feeding in the surface film. Some variety of hatching patterns will undoubtedly be necessary for coping with these trout, which are often feeding very selectively and even switching their selections from one specimen to another in the course of a single rise period, making identification a very difficult problem for the fisherman.

Just to diagnose the general situation is hard enough: and occasions for fishing in-surface are often not recognised at all. Rise forms don't help much: head-and-tail rises are particularly ambiguous—though the most likely guess about them might be the stuck nymph.

I describe in a later chapter the events of a wasted day when I vainly attempted by observation, as well as trial and error, to discover what fly the trout were rising to. I might have had a really exceptional catch if I had read the indications aright earlier than the last half hour, when I finally stumbled on the truth. Prejudice and the habit of persistence had frustrated me. That trout occasionally feed exclusively on hatching nymphs had never previously entered into my conscious experience.

Therefore, I view contemporary experiments in this area of fishing method with a very personal interest and hope. Now that I can moderate my desire for mere fish, the challenge of the hatching and stuck nymph appeals to me very strongly. Still water fishers, who have to cope frequently with midge-feeding trout, are being ably assisted. Representations of midge pupae, which float for long periods in the surface film, are becoming available—beautiful, lifelike imitations of tiny insects, products of the fly-tyer's art such as have never been surpassed. In-surface fishing, on both river and loch, is a very promising contemporary development. Though it may never become easy or popular because of limited applicability and inherent difficulty, it bids fair to become one of the more fascinating and challenging varieties of the sport.

Spinner-fall, the third occasion for it, is a common occurrence. Throughout the season it happens, on average, about once a day, though it may escape notice. In a failing light the rise form, when trout come up for spinners, is very inconspicuous, a mere dimpling of the surface. When trout show excitedly, they are more likely to be taking floating duns than spent flies. Thus an evening rise to spent flies may be undetected by the fisherman.

Even the trout may not see a spinner-fall, since it often takes place after dark. Trout feed by sight and, at night, only in that part of the season when the sky is not really dark and the flies available are larger than usual. Spinner-fall often occurs at dusk and may occasion, therefore, an evening rise. Sometimes trout will continue to feed on spent spinners of even the smallest flies long after the sun has gone down, if there is enough light in the sky to reveal them: but this is by no means usual. Spinner-falls sometimes occur in conditions of good visibility without any response from the trout, though I have no idea why. Thousands of flies, spread-eagled in the surface film, may drift round and round in the eddies completely ignored by the trout. Fishing in the surface film is not likely to be worthwhile on these occasions. But often enough trout are keen to make an easy meal off spent flies and it pays the angler to look out for these opportunities, which may occur at any time of day, though most typically in the evenings during warm weather.

He comes to a bend in the river, or a backwater aside from the main stream, and finds the surface dimpled with tiny rings. Obviously, fish are feeding on something in the surface layers. He may think them very small fish, but a few moments of observation will usually disabuse him of that notion. Often they are good trout, wasting none of their energy, but intent on making a steady meal off whatever is on the water.

They put their lips to the surface and draw in small mouthfuls of water along with their food. This makes tiny hollows in the calm surface with hardly any other disturbance. The trout for the most part are gliding a few inches under, and at an angle to, the surface, sipping here and there.

Because he sees nothing on the water the angler may think of nymphs or unhatched duns. Sometimes he succeeds in getting a pluck at representations of these, but is very unlikely to feel he has solved the mystery. If he persists in more than one or two casts, he only succeeds in putting the trout down.

I never failed in early years to be interested in this phenomenon and always had a go. Because it was a case of surface feeding, I would try dry fly, hatching nymph, and nymph in that order, but never had much success. Then one afternoon the river rose in sudden flood after a morning of torrential rain and I had no success with bait and no hope of fly fishing. I sat down beside a large eddy, where the current reversed itself, to drink a flask of tea and eat my bite. The eddy was fringed on the bank side with small items of flotsam and a collar of dirty foam. Between this and the strong main current the surface was quite smooth, circulating slowly.

The top two or three inches of the calm patch were almost clear; but lower down this transparency was lost in the thickening layers of silt-loaded water. Then I noticed the dimpling of the surface already described. I was on a high bank looking almost straight down. When I concentrated on the dimpled area I could see the trout coming up to the surface and sipping.

I hadn't yet seen their prey, but looking down into the debris on my side of the foam fringe I saw hundreds of tiny flies, floating on the surface with their wings flat out on either side of their dead bodies. In fact, it was not easy to see their wings at all.

In clearer water they would have been almost invisible by reason of their transparency.

The conclusion was instantaneous. The dimpling trout were taking spent spinners lying in the surface tension and rendered almost invisible because their transparent wings were not lifted up into the air. Since they were dead or dying, the trout had no need of haste in taking them, hence the leisurely sipping take.

Their very numbers encouraged exclusive feeding. Even if the trout noticed the angler's nymph or dry fly, the contrast of form and attitudes of these would operate against their acceptance. Perhaps, therefore, now that the secret was out, a representation of an appropriate spent spinner would have a better chance of success.

That day I had no spent spinner artificials with me. The best I could think of was to trim a hackled dry fly by cutting off all the fibres which fell below the hook shank. This would allow the fly to lie in the surface film instead of above it.

After a careful retreat from the bank I was presently able to try this experiment by means of an overland cast. I took two fish out of that particular slack and added one or two more by looking for other similar eddies elsewhere in the flooded stream. But it taught me to be prepared for dimpling trout in future.

Hackle-point tyings designed for such occasions have always been available and recent innovations, as I have suggested, are likely to prove specially valuable. If the fisherman makes his own flies, which is to be recommended, simple variations of normal methods will prove quite satisfactory and rather better than trimmed dry flies. Two iridescent cock hackles such as will let the light shine through their fibres may be tied on the hook so that the tips extend sideways from the shank. Or else the usual round-the-shank form of hackling may be separated into two bunches of fibres extending horizontally. Provided not too much fibre is bunched the fly should alight and swim satisfactorily. Badger, Dark Olive or Pale Olive are suitable varieties. Any Red Spinner recipe is likely to prove a suitable basis for a hackle-point fly. If a hackle is wound above the wings, as Halford recommended, only a single, or at most two turns, should be used so as not to lift the fly out of the surface film.

I make no special claim for my own dimpler-horizontal, which is no more than a parachute fly with the minimum turns of hackle.

The parachute effect insures flotation in the surface film, and the choice of body colour, which is specially important, attends to the question of what kind of fly. Dimpler-horizontals are good when trout are behaving as described above. They are also very useful during the evening rise, which is often occasioned by a spinner-fall at the end of a warm summer's day. But if the productions of others, more expert in entomology and fly tying, prove more successful than my simple efforts, no one will be more thankful than I.

PART III

Gear, Tackle, and Trim

[10]

Rod, Line, and Reel

I will go with you to Mr Margrove who dwells amongst the Book-Sellers in St Pauls Church-Yard, or to Mr Stubs near to the Swan in Golding-lane; they be both honest men, and will fit an Angler with what Tackling he lacks.   IZAAK WALTON

First, let your Rod be light, and very gentle.   IZAAK WALTON

The original Margrove & Stubs have been out of business for a number of years, but their successors have inherited their honesty. The novice fisherman, seeking his first outfit, will enjoy the best service. After a year or two they will expect him to return, not to complain of his original purchases, but to supplement them. As he progresses, they know he will acquire notions as well as, they hope, the money to indulge them. Then, what a deal of wise talk!—about prismatic or parabolic curvatures, tip-, middle-, or butt-actions—and a lot of sagacious wagglings and weighings in the hand. If the genuine Margrove & Stubs' tradition has been carefully sought out, the first buying, though it costs only a few pounds, will be as dependable for quality as the second, which may attain to fifty or more. Of course, there are other establishments of which the less said the better, not recommended among the booksellers nor at the pub where honest anglers still frequent.

The Rod

Mr Margrove may recommend a built cane rod and Mr Stubs may be inclined, gently, to push a glass fibre one. These gentlemen have their individuality. Neither will refuse to sell a greenheart, perhaps a good second-hand one, if you insist on it: but will be sure to mention the factor of weight and the shortage of straight-grained wood for replacement of inevitable broken tips. Mr Margrove is conscious of a century of experience behind his cane rods, whose qualities of power and action are capable of so many variations that every hand and every use can be satisfied. Mr Stubs won't deny this: but he is up with the times, and will assure you that some of the very latest glass fibre blanks are so much better than the rubbish that first invaded the market that he now has complete faith in this latest material. He will promise you extra-light weight and any form of action desired.

I agree with Stubs. If you haven't too much cash, start with the best of the latest. Old hands will argue about the effects of bending a hollow glass tube and the suddenness of its recoil, and so on. The fact is, a beginner won't notice: he'll get used to the instrument he has and will find glass excellent for his immediate purposes. By the time this book is published glass fibre rods may be challenged by carbon fibre products, or something else. Meantime, a learner will be well suited with glass. It is light, incredibly strong, imperishable. If you decide on a glass rod, let Mr Stubs know the kind of fishing you want to do. He will choose models of medium to quick action, very suitable for downstream wet fly and excellent for the shorter, quicker casting of upstream nymph and dry fly.

I regret the cane rod. All my rods, after the first and up to the last acquisition, were cane ones which I made myself. I was very proud of them, though none was perfect. Any rod made by an amateur is bound to be conditioned by the principle of un-certainty. Faith and hope are great helps. Mine were slightly too slow or slightly too fast in action—errors of judgement built in with the cane. A nine-foot, three-piece rod used to take me three weeks to make and another to complete. It consisted of eighteen slips of cane of equilateral section, glued one by one on to a triangular former and planed carefully to shape and taper, attempting an accuracy of sixty-fourths of an inch. The glue took a day to harden; so one slip was planed each night. Then the three pieces were built out of six slips each. After this three-week job, the pieces had to be cleaned up, cut to exact length, ferruled, and ringed. What a work of craftsmanship a built cane rod is!

Cane rods are crustaceans: that is, nearly all their strength is in their exo-skeletons. If anything has gone wrong at the pre-liminary design stage when dimensions are determined, or during the preparation of the several slips of cane, very little can be done to rectify it after the gluing up. That's why the trade are so careful in their choice of prototypes, whereas my prototype had to be the final product. Nevertheless, my rods were good tools and many a trout had cause to know it.

Perhaps I regret the (possible) passing of the cane rod because it frustrates my hopes of transforming the industry with a new technique. No one is likely now to be interested in my vertibrate-built cane invention. I discovered, accidentally, that it is not necessary for a built cane rod to have all its power on the outside. It is possible to prepare the equilateral section slips of cane more or less in the usual way but to glue them together with the hard skins inside, providing an alternative arrangement of three or six radial vertibrations. By this arrangement the rod would lose none of its power; and, when completed, minor, or even considerable, alterations in its action could be made by the simple process of planing the faces as desired. Alas, the vertibrate cane rod will never now challenge the crustacean model, which remains a magnificent tool for the angler, and a work of craftsmanship equal to anything in the history of the useful arts. No wonder Mr Margrove and I have a nostalgia for the built cane rod.

The Line

For good performance, line and rod must be carefully matched. The trade have now agreed on standard definitions. Every rod has a recommended size of line to match it and evoke its best performance. These sizes are defined as A F T M numbers. A trout fly rod is likely to require a line in the range A F T M 4 to 9 according to its power. Too heavy a line may overstrain the rod. One too light will fail to flex the rod and demand undue effort on the part of the caster. For some purposes, as for instance upstream nymphing, a lighter than standard line for the rod will be preferred for the sake of delicate presentation: in conditions of contrary wind or for the sake of long casting, a heavier than usual line may be advantageous. Many anglers have two spools to a reel to allow for these, or other, variations without having to carry a complete extra reel. For a beginning, until the angler discovers his special requirements, a single, general purpose line of the appropriate size for his chosen rod is quite adequate.

There are several sorts of line, besides differences in weight—level, single-taper, double-taper, forward-taper, floating, sinking, floating-cum-tip-sinking, and perhaps other varieties. Level lines

F

are the cheapest. The next cheapest are the single-taper. These are really half-lines of about 15 yards length instead of the usual 30 yards and excellent for the beginner. The advantage of the taper is in the gentler presentation of the fly. Fifteen yards is not enough line on a reel for most fishing: it has to be supplemented with backing which is a cheaper form of line used to give length and to fill up the reel. A half-filled reel does not behave properly in fishing: too much power is required to turn the drum, and rewinding is too slow.

A first line, therefore, should match the rod and be tapered, either single or double. It should also be a floating line. The experienced angler will perhaps one day want a sinking line, but for nine out of ten occasions the floater is the more suitable. In the old days an oiled silk line was a sinker in its natural state: it was greased when the angler had need for a floating line. Modern floating nylon lines, when kept clean, don't require any greasing. They float by a kind of effervescence built into their dressing and, although there are reactionary tendencies among some anglers who prefer silk, these self-floating vinyl-coated nylon lines are likely to supersede the older kinds. Nylon has one drawback. It is lighter than silk and therefore a nylon line has to be much thicker and offers more resistance to the wind than a silk one. On windy days, I confess, I sometimes sigh for my old silk. But this is a fair price to pay for other advantages.

A floating nylon line is easily lifted off the water for recasting. It does not easily become waterlogged or get "drowned" in the stream when a big fish goes deep. It facilitates on-surface and in-surface presentation without dragging the flies under. It is suitable also for most under-surface nymph fishing when extended by a suitable length of leader. Only for some of the very latest developments of presenting nymphs or lures right on the bottom, or very near to it, is a sinking line helpful or necessary. A beginner may safely postpone this need and be content with a floating tapered line as his main reel material.

There is a choice of colours available and not much to say about any. All lines are likely to be seen by the trout in silhouette against the light and will appear dark. An ivory or white line is very conspicuous to the eye of the angler and I would therefore recommend it. I was greatly amused one day last season. I met a fisherman who was very dissatisfied with his luck. He had seen me catch a couple of fish and had come up to chat about it. He examined my tackle and came to the conclusion that my white line was the secret. "I never know where my fly is," he said. "I'm getting blind. Yes, it's a white line for me next year." Among all the variables, I doubt if his diagnosis was correct: but, then, he may understand his own eyesight problem better than I can.

The line must fill the reel to give maximum help in casting or running a fish. A half-filled reel is worse than a nuisance. The main problem in filling a reel is to determine how much backing to use. It is necessary to proceed backwards, as it were, putting on the main line first and the backing on top, as much of the latter as will comfortably fill the reel without jamming the bars of the cage. After that the lines have to be run off on to a second spare reel or line winder: then run again on to a third reel or winder so that the backing is again on top. Finally, the backing and the main line are wound on to their own reel in this order. Extra special care must be taken to see that the backing is knotted securely to the spindle and that backing and line are neatly joined either by a varnished splice or by the ingenious pin knot, details of which are given in the next chapter. The whole process of filling the reel is rather tedious, especially if winders or spare reels are not to hand. Rolls of newspaper can serve as slow substitutes.

The backing line may be braided terylene or soft nylon mono-filament of 20–25 lb breaking strain. Both are rotproof. Nylon has two disadvantages. It is very elastic and tends to set in coils. To offset these it should be pre-stretched by attaching it to garden clothes poles or trees and suspending a brick from the middle of each length for a couple of hours at a time. Some anglers are careful enough to strip their reels and to stretch the backing at the waterside before beginning a day's fishing. This is to eliminate the elasticity and obviate the tendency of nylon, when wound on to the reel under the tension of a heavy fish, to bed down into its own coils and so become jammed or even exert so much side pressure on the walls of the spool as to distort them. I confess I neglect this precaution. I doubt the seriousness of the danger. No trout exerts more than a few ounces of power over the line in ordinary fly fishing. No doubt nylon filled sea-spinning reels are a very different proposition. I do, however, empty my reel occasionally at home and rewind it at uniform tension to get rid of any slack or tight spots that may have been caused in the course of fishing.

The Reel

Modern reels are beautiful instruments, simple and precise in their mechanism. They fascinate me and I tend to accumulate them. They consist of a drum revolving in a cage. There is nothing to catch or entangle the line except the handle, which is therefore as small and simple as possible, being attached, without crank, directly to the side plate of the drum. The turning of the drum is checked by a spring and pawl engaging a small toothed wheel. This provides the characteristic sound of the reel, which has become a sentimental feature of fly fishing, but more practically it prevents overruns and line entanglements. Such reels require little maintenance: periodic drying with a cloth and a touch or two of oil. There are more complicated models with variable checks, slipping clutches, exposed rims or gearing to allow of faster retrieve. These are harmless but no doubt heavier. You want the lightest possible reel. A narrow drum is the simplest and lightest form of gearing. So it's not necessary to be persuaded by Mr Stubs to go for anything very complicated unless you share his modern predilections. A word of warning, in case you have come by a second-hand reel (and why not?): older makes, designed for the thinner oiled-silk lines, may not have the capacity for full-size double taper nylon ones: though even these reels are likely to be suitable for the half-lines I have recommended for a beginning.

One persistent inconvenience, rooted in superstition, should be boldly abolished. Get a reel with left-hand wind. It is a lifelong mystery to me that anglers imagine they can't wind in with the left hand. Two minutes trial should convince anyone that left-hand winding is the only sensible way to do it. The rod, normally, is manipulated in the right hand. The left is free to adjust the length of line in use; and during fishing such adjustments are a constant job, not just when a fish is on, but at every other cast. The left hand shortens line by pulling it down through the rod rings, or it lengthens it by pulling extra off the reel, or it retrieves line in excess of immediate need by winding the reel. It is always busy. Fancy having to change the rod hand every time some winding in has to be done. So get a left-hand-wind reel. I used to have to alter my reels by moving the pawl and its spring to the other side of the spindle, a fairly simple rivetting job which, however, rather disfigures the side plate of the reel. Nowadays, Mr Stubs will provide you with a reel convertible for either hand. It will have a double pawl and spring. It's a simple matter to put one out of action and engage the other.

Another innovation, which Mr Stubs has introduced from the continent, is the self-wind automatic reel. I have not used one but would not like to be prejudiced against it. In course of fishing it often happens that a considerable amount of loose line is drawn off by the left hand. Whether this just hangs down on the water or is held in loops by the hand, it is a great embarrassment when a fish takes and, instead of running away and so drawing out the loose line, chooses instead to run towards you. Very often you lose that fish because you cannot maintain a tight line. It is useless trying to wind in the slack. All you can do is to increase the slack by pulling in more line by means of the left hand, in the hope that the trout will turn at last and take it out again. The automatic solves that problem. When a fish is hooked the loose line is dropped. A touch to the rewind lever causes it to be rewound instantly so that firm contact is maintained. The lever is kept depressed during the playing of a fish, any line stripped through the rings is automatically zipped in, and the reel allows line to be drawn off at any plunge or run by the fish. The rewind spring will zip back as much as 18 yards of line and can be set by the angler to suit his requirements. It is gentle enough for the finest end tackle the fly fisher is likely to use. Nevertheless, I am not convinced yet that its advantages offset the extra weight; furthermore, I would argue that a beginner would learn more easily with a manually operated reel what is involved in casting and playing. A self-wind automatic might reasonably be postponed. Perhaps, in any case, the last thing he wants is to over-mechanise the pleasures of fly fishing.

[11]

Gear, Gadgets and Gimmickry

Lord! How many things are there in this world of which Diogenes hath no need?
IZAAK WALTON

This chapter is something of a miscellany—more advice on equipment, a few tips and wrinkles on sundry difficulties, and finally some instruction in the useful art of knotting.

Waders

Even when fishing from the bank you will, occasionally, have to step into shallows to net a fish or unhook your fly from an obstruction. The best managed fisheries have ditches or wet meadows to cross. The nearest bridge may be a mile or more downstream when your car, or the pub, is just over the ford. Waders are sensible and necessary equipment.

There's a fair choice. Thigh length, lightweight, combined boots and waders are now favourites for small to medium waters. Felt soles make wading on gravel or rock very safe. They may be less reliable on wet grass or mud. Leather or composition soles, well studded with steel rivets, are still the best. Latex rubber between-waders have served me well for many years. They come to waist level and are yet easy to walk in. They are very reassuring to sit down on when the bank is wet with rain or dew. A mini puncture repair outfit is a useful accessory in case you are so careless as to push through gorse or sit on bramble thorns. Unfortunately they need brogues or over boots which are completely off the market. My present pair have been cobbled three times—almost rebuilt on the last. Another season will finish them. Outsize army boots, or some other resource, will be necessary; or else I'll have to conform to the majority and buy the combined article which is so easy to put on and off. There's at last a cheap form of incredibly light vinyl wader, also waist high, which I use on some expeditions as, for instance, when I go 1,200 feet up an Appin mountain to fish its fairy loch. The vinyl waders take up only a pocketful of space. They need proper brogues for the river, but an old pair of shoes is adequate for the loch on the ben.

Separate waders have to be cushioned by thick socks against abrasive grains of sand which, otherwise, would quickly cause leaks. Woollen socks had constantly to be darned, but that's a thing of the past. I've used a pair of nylon socks for at least four years now without maintenance.

Receptacle

Why carry bag, basket, or barrel (this last in Germany)? What's wrong with a jacket? A poacher's pocket may be fitted and lined with a removable plastic bag. You can pin your amadou wallet to the front, hang your little bottle of oil on a button, stick useful pins, or flies, in the lapel, and fill up the pockets with the rest of your essentials. What a heavy burden of superstition fishermen's receptables are! They were necessary when everything had to be carried from home to river—boots, waders, tackle, food, etc, etc. Now the car gets you there without burdens. From boot to bank, only what you stand up in is necessary. But remember to take your rod along as well. Of course, the etceteras tend to multiply.

I'm intrigued with a chic little importation from Japan—a fisherman's waistcoat, de luxe model. It has a lot of little and larger pockets. A ventilated pouch takes a few average trout: if you go in for fishmongering, you can make extra trips back to the car. You'll probably do this halfway through the day, anyhow. The waistcoat slips over your other garments and reaches down to waist level. I have modelled it happily on recent visits to the waterside where it has been greatly admired!

Dress for Women

It's not necessary in these days of unisex dress to make special recommendations about how women anglers should rig themselves out: whereas in 1895, writing in the Badminton Library volume on *Fishing: Salmon & Trout,* H Cholmondeley-Pennell took several pages to hail the advent of women to the sport:

> *"Fight on, brave knights! Bright eyes behold your deeds—"*

as if they did so just to admire the men. Nevertheless, he gave very serious advice for women fishers. "No skirts will vex the tameless ankles of our women of the future," he prophesied, more accurately than he knew. "There is a marked and healthy improvement visible in the length of the dress, and women need no longer draggle behind them a ridiculous and often muddy train." So much, and a lot more, as introduction to his specific recommendations: "Short skirt of linsey wolsey, made as simple as possible. . . . All wool undergarments should be worn, from stockings upwards. . . . Boots should lace in the same way that men's shooting boots do, and be made to come well up the leg (so that gaiters can be dispensed with)." Then, at last, he specifies: "Length of skirt—*an inch or so above the ankle.*" (My italics.) The bold man "made no apology for offering a few hints on the subject".

Landing Net

You can use your hand, as I often do, or a pair of tongs, as Arthur Wanless used to recommend; but a landing net is the best overall means of getting trout out of the water once they have been hooked and played. A small fly hook and a 3 lb nylon point are not dependable when you lose the protection of the Law of Archimedes. Collapsible nets are the handiest and work well; but they keep getting lost. They hang from a ring at the left, usually attached to the bag. When you kneel down, or clamber up a bank, the shaft pushes the clip upwards and off the ring, and the net lies down doggo on the bank or slips unobtrusively into the water. Dozens of times I have had to retrace hundreds of steps looking for the fugitive things, and I've lost three of them. To prevent such vexations, fix the ring well up under the left oxter on to the jacket itself, or by means of a strap passed over the right and under the left shoulder. In that position the net is just as easy to get at and its attempts to escape are frustrated.

See that the mesh is of hard, unbraded nylon or similar modern fibre. It will last indefinitely. Oiled silk or cotton is satisfactory but rots inwardly; it may let the fish of a lifetime drop through its bottom just when you are in no mood for philosophy. Hard cord—because barbed hooks form attachments for soft woven stuff. Why does the trade still supply the soft kind? I must have a word with Mr Stubs about it.

Scissors

By all means use your teeth to trim nylon ends. They won't need sharpening for about thirty years. Alas, my dentist crowned my own particular incisor and now I have to carry scissors. Teeth or scissors—you can't do without one or the other even if, like my lamented grandmother, you have "willing gums".

Glasses

We have seen that fly fishers are usually long-sighted. After about age fifty long-sighted people need glasses for reading or tying on flies. The latter is more important for fishing. Have your glasses handy, but safe. If, fumbling in midstream, you drop them, they become very inconspicuous at the bottom of the river and of no use to the trout, who are short-sighted.

Polaroid specs are a boon. They remove glare from the surface and sometimes make fish visible in the water. (I know another way to do that, which I discovered in Ireland. Pour all the surplus milk from a creamery into the river every day at five o'clock. For the next hour or so this turns the water, incredibly, a lovely shamrock green, in which every trout becomes mysteriously and beautifully visible, fairy fish in an elfin wonderland, and, what's more, ready to feed on anything offered to them by an angler's fairy wand.) But about polaroids—flip-ups are specially good. They can be worn continuously on days of shadow and shine, turned up or down according to need.

Priest

As you love them, always cudgel your fish neatly on the head. Pick up a blunt instrument from under the trees in the morning and carry it in your waist band. You'll probably still have it in the evening when there's no need to take it home. Or you can buy an expensive little priest made of aluminium which you'll probably lose. Tether it.

Clothing

A lightweight waterproof jacket, long enough to hang over the tops of your waders, is necessary for this climate; and a hat of similar material to shed the rain, though some men prefer cloth or knitted headgear, which absorbs a surprising amount of water. This is exceptional: fishermen don't, as a rule, absorb much water.

Tips

A plastic bag put on under a leaky wader prevents that foot-in-a-watery-grave feeling.

A bit of adhesive cloth tape has many uses, such as fixing loose ferrules or as first aid for rod or person.

A tiny cloth pad soaked in detergent quickly removes grease from nylon or flies. Floating nylon (its only fault) is conspicuous in the surface film and encourages drag.

A fine file or, better, small hone slip, allows hook points to be touched up now and then. It won't mend broken hooks or find lost ones: so keep an equally sharp lookout. When trout stop rising it may be you're offering them only a nylon point which won't hurt them even if they see it.

Avoid garish clothing or hard shiny surfaces. Beards are good camouflage for the young.

A spare set of essential clothing, bagged in polythene and always in the boot, will one day save you from a wet drive home.

Don't fall into the river. If you do, don't panic. Your waders will buoy you up if full of air; and the story that they force your head under water was exploded in 1867. You can swim in waders quite easily, if slowly, even when they're full of water, for the simple reason that water is of the same specific gravity whether inside or out. Better than swimming, just walk decisively downstream, if you're on your feet, and into the side as soon as possible. You'll do it on your toes like a ballet dancer. If you have to go over a cauld or a weir, which should only happen in books, feet first is the better way. Don't wade across a rising river if you've to get back again. Whenever you wade in strong water, edge your way, sideways to the current, with one foot always firmly planted. Keep off the tops of large underwater boulders: it's hard to get down again. Always use a wading staff on the Scottish Dee (it's a better weapon against any enemy than your rod) and the utmost care anywhere else. Hydraulic power causes other misfortunes besides expensive electricity. Don't wade where you're going to fish, and remember the other fellow who hasn't yet spoiled the pool for you. Even if he does, there's no need to take it out on yourself.

KNOTS

Security of mind and tackle depends on the fisherman's proficiency in tying knots. He will never equal the perverse facility of a squally wind, but his creations will serve useful purposes and only minimally reduce the strength of his tackle, whereas wind knots are products of a malicious and destructive devil. It is necessary to learn only a few reliables which have been tested to conserve more than 85 per cent of the original strength of the material involved. They should be practised till they almost tie themselves, whatever the conditions.

Turle Knot for attaching eyed flies. The single turle may do for very small hooks (18–20) and finest nylon. Thread nylon through eye and run hook up out of way. Bend nylon in loop below fly and tie loose thumb knot, thus:

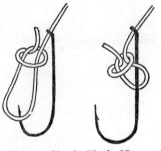

Fig. 4 Single Turle Knot

I don't trust the single turn for larger hooks. I double the thumb knot by taking the free end round the standing part again and in and out of the knot already made following the original route. The result look like this:

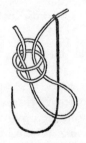

Fig. 5 Double Turle Knot

Then I lubricate the knot and draw it tight. The hook is next run down into the loop which is drawn tight round the neck under the eye. Test for tightness and snip off the spare end. About lubrication: a friend of mine, who always votes left, says, "Saliva's good, but spit's better." Nowdays you just can't keep politics out of sport.

This double turle has *never* failed me.

Pin Knot for joining line and nylon monofilament, easier than a splice and not inferior.

Insert a pin into hollow end of the line and bring point through the side about quarter of an inch from the end. Heat the head of pin in a match flame until red hot. This keeps tube and hole open. Remove pin. (If you didn't cool it first you'll wish you had.)

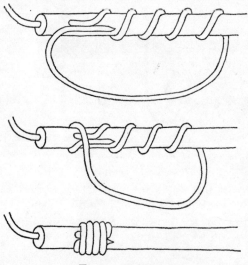

Fig. 6 Pin Knot

(1) Push end of nylon into line, bringing several inches through hole.

(2) Wrap nylon loosely round and up the line four (or more) turns. These are temporary turns. Lay end of nylon alongside line with end pointing up line.

(3) Bind down the laid end of nylon with four (or more) turns of its own strand, making these permanent turns in the

reverse direction from that of the temporary turns which are thus undone. These permanent turns start just above the hole and are laid close together, again up the line.

(4) Pull end and main length of nylon alternately to tighten knot. The turns will bed down into the resilient line making a very secure union.

Shooting head specialists and tournament casters may remove the dressing from the end of the line first and whip and varnish the knot afterwards to make its passage through the rod rings even smoother; but for ordinary fishing purposes I find this unnecessary.

Blood Knot. This sinister ingenuity is the angler's best friend. Properly made it will not let him down. No other knot is so adaptable to different purposes or retains so high a degree of strength in the nylon.

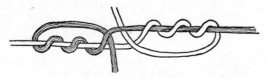

Fig. 7   Blood Knot

Lay the two strands to be joined alongside each other with enough free ends to do the tying. Hold strands in middle between pads of thumb and forefinger. Wrap each end, one at a time, over the longer standing part for three or more turns. The ends should go round in opposite directions. Then insert the ends, from opposite sides, through the centre of the knot (which has been held open between the fingers). The knot may now be released, lubricated, and drawn tight by slow pulling on the long strands. To assist closure the turns may be pressed against each other with the nails of thumb and forefinger. When making the two halves of the knot you will have to transfer it from one hand to the other as the disengaged hand makes the separate set of turns. As a third hand, I use my teeth to pull the ends through the centre. Perhaps you'll have to do the same. To be sure of a proper sequence of operation I sing a little song to myself as I tie this knot:

Song of the Blood Knot

Up the front, down the back,
Up the front, down the back,
Up the front, down the back,
And in from the front.

Down the front, up the back,
Down the front, up the back,
Down the front, up the back,
And in from the back.

To make a blood knot quickly and firmly is a necessary skill for every angler. It becomes easy with practice.

It is always difficult if the two strands are of markedly different gauges. When you can't get a thick and thin strand to form a normal blood knot use a

Blood Fisherman's Knot.

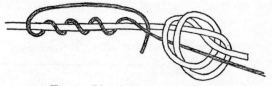

Fig. 8 Blood Fisherman Knot

Tie a double-turle at the end of the thick strand. Pass thin strand through this knot and draw knot really tight. Then make a half-blood with thin strand around the thick one, bringing the free end out between the two strands in the middle. Pull both main strands to draw knots together, lubricate and pull really tight.

Droppers can easily be provided in both these cases by leaving one long free end sticking out from the knot. For security of tackle, the dropper should be an extension of the *upper* strand.

Jam Knot, for attaching leader to line. Make a loop at head of leader by a double thumb knot, thus:

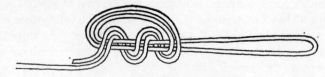

Fig. 9 Double Thumb Knot

Tie single thumb knot at end of reel line and pass through loop, round and under the loop, and finally under its own standing part:

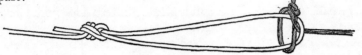

Fig. 10   Jam Knot

When closed the jam knot will not slip. It will be conspicuous on the water and so may help to keep the position of leader and flies in view during fishing. But it is just a little cluttersome and tends to collect floating algae or catch on herbage. The loop at the head of the leader is the only one permissible in fly fishing. Loops are clumsy and advertise the tackle to the sensitive eye of the trout. I long ago discarded the loop and jam knot. Instead I pin knot a short strand of nylon to the end of the reel line. The leader is attached to this strand by an ordinary blood knot, the top of the leader being of the same, or very similar, gauge as the connecting strand.

Gadget for Tying Blood Knots

You need three hands and a lot of fingers to tie reliable bloods. Here, then, is a simple contraption to supplement nature. The materials are easy to come by—two spring clothes pegs, a 2½-inch round nail, two small bits of rubber, and some instant cement. The diagram should make the construction clear.

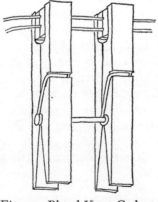

Fig. 11   Blood Knot Gadget

First, reduce the inside gripping surfaces of the pegs with a chisel or file and stick on the rubber pads to provide firm holding surfaces. Join the pegs through the holes in the springs with a large nail. The neck of the nail is already burred and should grip one peg quite firmly. Use a tack hammer and burr the shank lower down until it grips the second peg. There should be a gap of half to three-quarters of an inch between the pegs. Cut off the protruding end of the nail and the gadget is made. Alternatively, instead of using a nail, the pegs could be held apart by a strip of wood fastened to their lower backs; but the nail is perhaps easier.

The use of this little contraption is simpler than its construction. To tie a blood knot in nylon, overlap the ends to be joined and grip the two strands, separated by a slight space, between the jaws. Leave the ends long enough to push through the middle of the knot. A match or a small nail can be used as a lever to make the turns, three or more, depending on the gauge of the nylon or your own ideas of security. Then bend over each end in turn and insert through the knot on each side of the lever, making sure that they go through from opposite sides. This is easily arranged by making a further half turn with the lever before inserting the second end. Wet the knot to assist tightening and pull the two long strands. It will close beautifully. Withdraw the lever, remove the knot from the gadget, and complete the tightening. A little practice and it is goodbye to all fear of badly made blood knots and the losing of fish they lead to.

A purist may point out that the knot it makes is not a pure blood since both right and left turns are made in the same direction: provided the ends are put through the centre from opposite sides the impure result is just as reliable.

Perhaps I should put out a warning, in case anyone sees a chance of easy money by pirating my gadget: that it was not designed to make a fortune but to make blood knots. There are expensive knotting machines now on the market. Besides, as you pay for the health service in any case, you should find fingers and teeth cheaper even than clothes pegs, and my little gadget may be worth no more than a pocketful of fun at the beginning of your fishing career.

PART IV

Technique

G

[12]

Casting

I lend you indeed my Fiddle, but not my Fiddlestick. IZAAK WALTON

We live in a very practical age. Writers hesitate to describe what is more easily demonstrated. Education itself, at least in its primary stages, exploits the activity rather than the academic approach even to subjects that develop far into regions of abstract thought. It is a healthy instinct that makes a man prefer an evening or week-end course in casting a trout fly to reading about it in a book. Such courses are advertised in angling magazines and by the tackle trade. They cost a small expense for a considerable saving of time and vexatiousness.

Yet education is facilitated by mental preparedness. To consider what casting is all about, the basic principles of the skill and the several varieties of it, is helpful. The mind rules the body and works as much in secret as in consciousness. A sure way of acquiring a skill quickly is to set the mind working on it, organising the physical processes that underly it. Reading and thinking about the job before and during practice of it help to work the miracle every skill is. Thus I write about casting less to teach it than to give the angler's mind something to work on in preparation for the real job of his learning to cast. I lend him my fiddle, indeed. He must use his own fiddlestick.

Short rods and long lines have made casting a necessary skill. We cannot lay our flies on the water under the tip of the rod, or depend on the wind to present them farther astream. We manipulate a long stiffish spring to propel them. A fly rod is not a whip, though it will behave like one if that's what you imagine, making the line crack deliciously in the air and your expensive flies disappear mysteriously from the end of it. *You* are not casting a line: the rod is. *You* are wielding the rod. You, the rod, the line—

in that order. Master the rod and it will manage the line. You master the rod best if you understand it as an extension of your arm. Thought and practice will make it behave, with all its tensile power, as if it were a natural part of your musculature. It is an instrument of power, not a thing to wave about nervelessly; a thing to bend into use. Every time it bends it stores energy to be released immediately after. This released energy casts the line. You start the process by bending the rod into use at the beginning of each cast. You bend the rod: the rod casts the fly. That's it.

The Basic Cast

Most forms of casting have the same basic form. The only real difference is in the plane of cast which may be at any required angle—vertical, oblique, horizontal. The basic cast is best learnt in the vertical plane. The rod works in front of and over the casting shoulder, usually the right.

To present line and fly across the water requires not one but two casts, a back cast and a forward one. A distinct and important pause separates the two rod movements. If it is omitted the line will crack like a whip lash with results already described.

Let us analyse these casts. Paradoxically, we start from a position at the end of a successful forward cast. The line is extended across the water (or field). The rod is held horizontally pointing forwards to the nine o'clock position of an imaginary clock face. The hand holding it is relaxed. At no time need muscles be more than half taut.

THE BACK CAST

Lift: That is, loosen the line from the water by raising the rod from nine o'clock to about ten-thirty.

Drive: Continue and accelerate the lift movement by bending the elbow, keeping forearm, wrist and rod in line, until the rod is pointing to twelve or one o'clock. This drive flexes the rod as it pulls the heavy line away from the water and starts it travelling backwards, unrolling as it goes.

Pause: That is, check the rod decisively at one o'clock. At the pause the rod will spring back to the straight and propel the line backwards the way it is already going, until it is stretched straight. After a few trials you will acquire

enough confidence to turn the head during the pause and
watch the line unfold.

FORWARD CAST

Drive: The forward drive pulls the line and again flexes the rod.
Pause: The drive is checked again decisively between ten and
eleven o'clock. The rod imparts its energy to the line
which rolls and unrolls forward in the air until it is again
stretched out straight.
Lower: During the pause the tip of the rod may come down to the
nine o'clock horizontal position again. Then you lower
arm and rod as the line settles down on the water with the
fly at its extremity. If comparatively short, line and leader
will lie down at almost the same time. If long, the heavier
nearer section will reach the water first and the lying down
will proceed continuously outwards until the fly completes
the action.

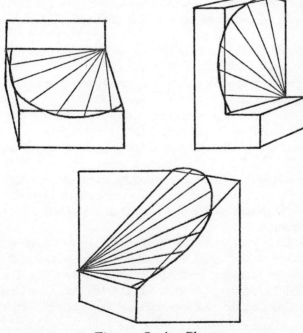

Fig. 12 Casting Planes

The whole basic cast may be summarised, and should be rehearsed mentally, as follows:

Back-cast: Lift—drive—pause.
Forward-cast: Drive—pause—lower.

Most other casts are variations on the above, the main difference being in the plane of operation. The rod cuts a swath of air, rather more than a quarter of a circle in size, as it passes from the horizontal nine o'clock to the one o'clock positions. Imagine a semicircle of cardboard, marked with the time positions, balanced vertically on a dummy angler's right shoulder. That's the area in which the rod operates. The line at each of its opposite extensions defines the diameter of the semicircle. The cardboard can be imagined pivoted in other positions to illustrate other casts— horizontally to the right or left, obliquely across the chest and over the left shoulder.

Some anglers make a practice of imparting a slight lift to the back cast—steepling it—to prevent the hook catching on the ground behind. Some alter the planes of the back and forward casts to avoid collisions between line and rod. The rod is held slightly oblique at the back throw and more truly vertical at the forward one. Collisions do occur, mainly on windy days and when casts are made from a deep wading position.

The mental preparation advocated above will simplify practice. Hand and arm have to work as parts of the rod: the muscles remain half relaxed: and the movements of the rod accelerate smoothly from lift to pause and from drive to pause. As with most physical skills, timing is of the essence which comes as a knack. Once acquired the knack is never lost and adjusts to varying conditions. Casting is delightful exercise.

Here are a few notes on the main casts used in fly fishing.

Over-right-shoulder or *Vertical Cast*. Described above. All others derive from it.

False Casting. A series of back and forward casts without presentation on the water. Useful for whisking water off line and dry fly or for extending line. The length of line aerialised may be shortened by drawing down with the left hand between the bottom ring and the reel and releasing this gathered line at the forward drive's moment of maximum power, when it shoots out again through the rings. False casting, in this way, is greatly

Fig. 13   Vertical Cast

speeded up and causes less fatigue. To extend line during false casting, line is stripped from the reel by the left hand as the back drives are made until the angler judges he has enough out to reach his target, when the cast may be taken to its final lowering stage. False casting is often much overdone but is a useful trick. Best not do it over a trout, reserving only the final cast of a series for that honour.

Over-left-shoulder or Oblique Cast. Not the only oblique one possible, but the most valuable. It is the right-handed angler's standby when fishing upstream from the left bank. It helps him to fish neglected, and therefore, profitable areas close to the left bank, or to cheat a downstream wind which causes collisions between line and rod with the basic cast. Like the backhand drive

Fig. 14   Oblique Cast

in tennis, it tends to lack power, and is tiring when continued over long periods until the muscles are trained.

Side or Horizontal Cast. The plane is parallel to the water or the bank. Normally the back drive is lower than the forward one to avoid collisions. It may be to the right or left. Its chief purposes are to avoid overhead obstructions, to keep rod movements out of sight of trout, and to cheat the wind which is usually weaker nearer the surface. It is hazardous over shaggy banks and comes into its own over water.

Shepherd Crook Cast. A horizontal cast designed to cause the point of the leader to fall on the water in a decided curve, so that the fly will float down ahead of the leader and thus be more likely to deceive a trout. An ordinary horizontal cast sometimes effects this, especially if a slight downstream wind helps to make the crook or curve. It is facilitated by making the horizontal cast underhand, that is, making the forward throw on a lower plane than the back throw. If the cast is made on the angler's right the

Fig. 15 Horizontal Cast

curve will occur to the left, which is the usual requirement when fishing upstream and towards the right bank. If the cast is made from the left, the crook will occur to the right, which is useful when fishing up and towards the left bank. These crook casts are always a bit chancy: wind may help, but more often it ruins the attempt. It's good fun practising crook casts when the trout are dour. A typical occasion for the use of a crook cast is mentioned in the chapter on Sunshine/Shadow Strategy.

Steeple Cast. To avoid rear obstructions, as when casting from the base of a high bank. If the back cast is made upwards by raising the whole arm at the moment of drive, instead of just bending the elbow, the line will go almost straight up. The forward drive is as usual, but sometimes the impact with the water is more violent than ideal.

Spring or *Bow Cast.* Useful among trees or bushes which make other casts impossible. Enough line is drawn out from the top

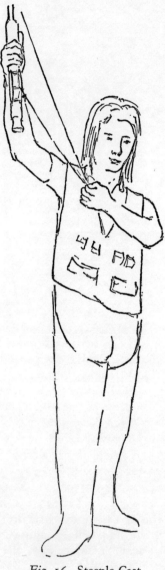

Fig. 16 Steeple Cast

ring to reach the target, which must be a near one. The fly is held by the left finger and thumb and the rod extended towards the target. A certain amount of judgement based on experience is necessary here. Then the rod is flexed by pulling on the line. When the fly is released the spring of the rod propels the line out and, with luck, the fly alights near enough to the spot desired.

Shooting the Line. Already described under false casting. Special weight-forward, torpedo-form lines are designed to facilitate long casting by this method: but the ordinary tapered line permits it quite satisfactorily for most purposes. Shooting line at every cast is good practice: it ensures gentler presentation. The drive has to be strong enough to take all the shoot out. The double-haul, a much discussed part of contemporary casting development, is advanced technique for increasing air-speed and getting extra long lines out across the water. I am no expert at this and would recommend the curious reader to Charles Ritz's *Fly Fisher's Life,* second edition, for full details by the originator.

Roll or Spey Cast. Another, rather more difficult method of avoiding rear obstructions, borrowed from salmon fishing practice on the heavily timbered banks of the river that gives it a name. It is very suitable for upstream fishing. The fly is projected in the required direction by a rolling action of the line which never really loses touch with the water: in fact the drag of water is necessary for its efficient execution and it cannot be done well in the practice field. The line does not pass to the rear of the angler at all. It is effected as follows. From its extended position the line is brought back across the body of the angler, in a large curve by means of a slow, gradual raising of the rod usually towards the left shoulder. Then, by a decided hammer blow of arm and rod in the desired direction, the line is made to turn over itself in a roll that travels swiftly over the water carrying the fly along with it. When the roll straightens out the fly hits, or falls on, the surface. It's an excellent cast for changing direction. For instance: imagine you are facing across stream and wish to place the fly straight across but cannot use a back or steeple cast. You may cast upstream to your right first: then, drawing the line down and across your front as described above, make a roll cast straight across. In this way you effect a right-angled change of direction and may reach trout otherwise unreachable.

To the above may be added the self-explanatory

Overland Cast. Used when an approach to the water's edge would alert the trout. Most of the line is extended over the top of the bank from the landward side, the leader and fly falling on the water. Extra allowance for the height of the bank must be estimated or else the fly will alight short of target. If the fish is not hooked, the retrieve is a slow withdrawal of line by means of the left hand, or occasionally, by raising the rod, depending on the hackle of the fly to shield the bend of the hook. As often as not the herbage will not catch. Thereafter, the cast may be repeated, perhaps more accurately and with better result.

Off the Bank. The overland cast is associated in my mind with a special form of presentation used to get at a trout hugging the opposite bank. The fisherman deliberately casts on to the opposite bank and gently draws on the line, or allows the current to do so, till the fly falls from the bank on to the water above the fish. It's risky, of course, but the fisherman who doesn't take risks will miss many opportunities. It's also, sometimes, sheer magic.

Casts made from the bank will generally be from a kneeling position. Standing gives greater distance but seldom enough to reach unalerted fish. When wading the angler has less obstructions to avoid and, because of his low position, less need of long casts. It should be a rule to keep them as short as possible. Only when they are very short, as in fishing up a stickle with the dry fly, will the left hand be unemployed, contact with fly being maintained by raising the rod tip as the fly drifts back. But rises will be missed if the rod is raised too near the vertical, since it cannot be moved through sufficient angle at the strike to tighten line and set the hook. It is best to keep such casts very brief, never raising the rod higher than an angle of 45° to 60°. The left hand is the right hand's best friend, lessening fatigue and making for positive strikes. It gathers in line as the fly is borne down the current. The left hand may pull the gathered line out to the side to the full stretch of the arm, releasing it at the next forward drive. Or, if there is too much of it for that manoeuvre, it may be allowed to fall, as it is drawn through the rings, on to the water beneath the hand, or gathered in small coils, or figure-of-eight folds, in the hand. The coils or folds are released successively at the shoot. Practice makes perfect. Coiling or folding is almost always necessary when long casting from the bank, since lawn conditions are rare and loose line inevitably tangles with the plants and debris.

Finally, some words about wind. It upsets all attempts at perfection. An upstream wind may help to take your flies up for you, but at a greater risk of cracked-off flies at the back cast: so use this wind carefully; less drive is necessary. A downstream wind, if not too strong, is often better for raising flies and, therefore, trout; but, beyond a certain force, it may ruin vertical casting from the left bank. The answer to this wind is to fish from the right bank, so as to get maximum power from horizontal casting with the right hand. Young anglers should make it an objective to become ambidextrous: whatever bank they are on they can, then, make use of their downstream hand and cut their casts in under the wind horizontally. Gusty weather is better than continuous strong wind. When gusts attack, you await a lull before retaliating. Lulls between gusts are usual and allow you to get at least some of your own back. Incidentally, keep examining your leader: wind knots are a serious cause of breakages. A shorter, heavier leader is advisable for stormy weather and the ruffled surface makes it no disadvantage *vis-à-vis* the trout.

Often the best policy is not to fight the wind. Casting across rather than against it, preferably with the downstream hand, is often surprisingly easy. This hand is important, making collisions between line and rod impossible, since a sudden gust at the time of casting will blow the line downstream away from the rod, rather than against it. Gusts may frustrate some casts but cause no other inconvenience. If the downstream wind is too strong even for across-stream casting, there is little alternative to turning the back on it and working downstream either with wet or dry fly, of which more anon.

Casting is a fascinating game, well worth thought, study, and practice. It becomes reflex action, like all skills. Exercising it in difficult conditions gives a sense of achievement. In ideal conditions it is one of the finest pleasures in the happy art of angling.

Fine and Far Off

To fish fine and far off is the first and principal Rule for Trout Angling.
CHARLES COTTON.

As long as casting continues to be a problem to the fisher, he has little freedom of mind to attend to other problems. However carefully he reads the water and selects the direction and distance to be cast, if he cannot reach his target accurately and neatly, he is not really fishing. In this sense, therefore, casting is a necessary and preliminary skill: as soon as it is acquired, and can be exercised habitually, with the minimum of conscious attention, he can begin to concentrate on the other variable factors and circumstances that make fly fishing such an absorbing interest. Casting problems never disappear: but they tend to be limited in variety and difficulty: whereas fly fishing, though it can indeed be practised in limited rule-of-thumb fashion by some anglers, promises the imaginative and enterprising angler an inexhaustible supply of fascinating experiences. Many of these can be anticipated by reading angling literature, which helps him to recognise situations and circumstances: but nothing really enables him to avoid experience itself. In the course of a lifetime of fishing he will learn a great deal, and if he keeps abreast of theory and maintains an experimental attitude he will acquire skill and enhance the pleasure of his sport. Experience is all. In the next three chapters I exemplify the kind of problems that lie immediately beyond the casting stage of learning and discuss typical ways of surmounting them.

It is appropriate to start with "the first and principal rule for trout angling" that Cotton compressed into four inspired words, whose validity has not been affected by three hundred years of angling history. A chapter on the text of "fine and far off" is too short to exhaust the wisdom it contains: but it will serve to reveal some of its implications for contemporary fly fishing.

The basic reasons for the policy are fairly obvious. Most fish, and trout especially, take fright at the sight of a moving human figure on the bank. They are made suspicious by clumsy tackle. These basic reasons are strengthened in calm, bright conditions and still more so when slanting light casts shadows. The shadow of a moving figure alerts a trout and may send it scurrying for shelter. The shadow of the line will alert it no less. Fine and far off is designed to avoid or minimise all these disadvantages.

The second part of the policy—far off—has another justification. In fact, it is a consequence of the first part. If you use a fine nylon point, a long cast is excellent insurance against breakage. The violence of a take is cushioned both by the water and by the inevitable slack in the line.

There are two by-product advantages. A useful and often necessary pause between take and strike is provided for by the time it takes for the angler's reaction to register at the end of his line. Furthermore, the longer line almost certainly engages the spring of the rod so that it, too, operates as a give to the pull of the fish. Thus there is increased certainty of the hook taking hold and the tackle bearing the strain of an unexpectedly large fish.

There are two qualifications of this. The angler's reactions may be too slow, in which case he might improve his success in striking by shortening line. He might also be wise to avoid too fine nylon. Secondly, he must use his rod to best advantage. I often watch spinners winding in with rod and nylon extended in a straight line out into the stream. Of course, they can rely on the slipping clutch of their reel. Even so, I think they'd improve both their technique and their pleasure if they kept an angle between rod and line so that the spring of the rod would come into play in event of a take.

For the fly fisher, even if he leaves his line free to run when a fish takes, this angle between rod and line is essential. True, there is a certain elasticity in nylon, but a nine-foot leader does not give enough of it for safety.

There is a specially dangerous period in the fishing-out of a long cast; namely, when the line comes round below one in a strong stream. There is no slack, and the rod may be almost straight with the line which draws directly on the reel. A heavy take at this moment often means a break. One tactic for this emergency is to transfer the angle between rod and line to another plane. As the horizontal angle straightens out, the rod point should be raised so as to make a vertical one. This provides a curve of slack line between rod and water and ensures the use of the rod's spring. Hand off the reel or line is a further safeguard. The largest sea-trout I ever hooked was lost by failure to practise these precautions.

The whole policy can never be a hard and fast one. It must be one of judgement. The angler must fish just as fine and far off as is necessary and always within the limits of his skill and his instruments. Beginners are often obsessed with the idea that long casting is good fishing, as if trout always live at the far side of a stream or halfway across a loch. They tend, therefore, to overreach their own powers and lose control of their tackle.

They wonder why they miss so many rises, blaming the trout instead of their own technique, or why they lose so many of those that hook themselves because their lines get drowned in heavy water. The policy must be varied according to the rod, the person, and the circumstances.

The thoughtful angler learns from experience and soon acquires a special sense that tells him just how far off to present his enticements to be successful. Short of this optimum distance will normally be useless; beyond it an unnecessary expenditure of effort. Of course, as he fishes, the distance keeps extending or contracting according to current, ripple, water clarity, or other circumstances. On a loch it may be kept constant for long periods of time, whereas on a river the circumstances are much more variable.

Too fine and far off, then, can be dangerous. I find that wet-fly fishing and nymphing normally require finer leaders than dry fly. Perhaps the reason is that the fly is presented *in* the water, the trout's own medium, where the attachments can more easily be detected, whereas the dry fly is more or less outside the trout's world. I surmise, too, that a trout inspects a wet fly more closely than a dry fly. It must often rise to the latter without having had time to examine it, taking it on the impression. Since the attention of the trout is aimed at a silhouetted shape beyond the surface layer it may easily fail to notice even quite substantial attachments.

In practice I can use three-pound nylon for most of my wet-fly fishing, but for dry fly I prefer four-pound material. Normally I make much shorter casts with the floating fly and, since there is little or no water cushion, breakages are more likely, hence the stronger cast.

In considering the conditions suitable for the policy it is necessary to take into account the mechanical properties of any particular rod. The breaking strains mentioned above may not suit other rods at all. The angler must know his rod, as I have come to know mine, and work within its limits. The trend is towards shorter rods. But casting is only part of a rod's function. Modern spinning rods may be quite short, but fly rods have still to be long enough to give the angler control after the cast has been made.

I have two final points. The first concerns size and power of fish. Fine nylon is good for increasing the number of offers, but it has resulted in many fish going off with hooks in their mouths and yards of nylon streaming in their wake. It's criminal to use too fine tackle. Unfortunately, many anglers take undue pride in their ability to fish fine and are careless about their inevitable failures.

The second point concerns the nature of the water. Where weeds or other obstructions abound, fine casts are folly. I had to experiment rather expensively about this on a recent holiday. I was spinning for sea-trout in a West Highland sea loch. I waded at various stages of the tide among the knotted wrack along the shore. When the tide was well in and the fish were among the tangle, or within easy reach of it, I had to use twelve-pound breaking strain. With this I could get two pounders or more to the net without losing them in the forest of weed, and if the spoon got caught up I could usually pull it free. Anything finer meant lost fish and tackle. At the ebb, when I was wading beyond the wrack with nothing worse than a long stringy sort of weed to deal with, I was able to use nylon as fine as six or seven pounds.

It took me a couple of days of broken ends and lost fish before I adapted my policy to the fishing conditions. Such experiment is always necessary before an angler becomes skilled enough to practice the policy of fine and far off with due regard for all the factors of rod, fish, and water conditions.

H

[14]

Sunshine/Shadow Strategy

*This day proves so calm, and the sun rises so bright, as promises no great
success to the Angler.*   CHARLES COTTON

It is unwise to dogmatise about anything connected with fishing.
The fish always have the last word and sometimes they confound
even our pessimism. Nevertheless, bright cloudless weather is
notoriously bad for fly fishing. The trout retreat to the deeps or
into the shade where they are hard to reach. The surface of the
water where we hope to see indications of activity becomes a
silver shield. The whole river seems dead. Unless a breeze springs
up or clouds intermit the glare the whole day may pass without
incident. In summer, when the temperature has been high, even
the hope of an evening rise, when the sun goes down and the
air cools, may be frustrated by a smoking mist.

Happily such conditions are seldom experienced in extreme
form. Wind or cloud may alleviate the unfavourable circumstances; at intervals flies may rise and trout come on the feed;
and the evening rise may actually fulfil the fisherman's fondest
hopes. Yet, bright conditions, even when they are modified from
time to time, present special difficulties.

On most rivers there are places where the trout can escape the
glare—under overhanging trees, bushes, or even undercut banks.
These places are difficult to fish: but by accepting the challenge
the fisherman will learn a lot and may achieve quite considerable
success. This is a time for working up close to a shady bank,
presenting nymph or dry fly right in the shadow, sometimes
allowing the current to carry it under overhanging lumps of earth
or bushes. The risk of getting hung up must be accepted. On
small streams there are sometimes tunnels between trees, seldom
fished, but where trout retreat to in hot bright weather. The fly

may have to be floated down. Rises are hard to strike; fish may be lost, and tackle too.

Dibbing with a natural or artificial insect (bluebottle, caterpillar grasshopper, or bushy dry fly) used to be common practice of country anglers in high summer. For some reason, visiting anglers seldom practise it nowadays, though it can be recommended as an interesting diversion for special occasions. It is a means of enticing the largest trout. The suspense that grips the fisherman as he lowers the fly and awaits the trout's interest is only equalled by the predicament he finds himself in when the fish takes and he has to manoeuvre it out of the water and through the ramifications of the trees. It can be a very exciting sport.

On most days, however, anglers will find it possible to fish by the more usual methods, provided they take extra special care not to advertise themselves to the watchful trout. Just because the conditions are difficult they will perhaps enjoy the exercise of special skills. It is appropriate to discuss these conditions in some detail.

"Nothing frightens trout more than moving shadows. In strong slanting sunlight the angler should choose, if possible, to face the sun so that his shadow falls behind him."

Although not quoted from any particular book on fishing, most anglers will recognise this as typical advice. It is good advice, as far as it goes, especially for beginners. But my object is to discuss the problems of light and shadow in somewhat greater detail and to suggest that this rule of thumb is just a little too simple, at least for more advanced anglers. The advice I am about to offer may seem heterodox, but I can quote one excellent contemporary authority to support it.

In the new edition of *A Fly Fisher's Life*, Charles Ritz gives this advice on fishing the evening rise: "As soon as day declines . . . take up a position on the bank with the light behind you, which is the only way of watching the presentation and the taking of your fly."

First consider the angler's point of view. If he is fishing into the light, everything coming between him and the sun tends to be in silhouette, without detail. This applies to any break on the surface of the water. A ripple or a rise will be a dark lump on the water. Often the one cannot be distinguished from the other and a rise may be missed. Peering into the sun is quite painful and very indiscriminating. Between the angler and the westering sun there is likely to be a blinding pathway across the water into which a floating fly just disappears. The angler will find himself craning his neck first to one side and then to the other to shorten the "blind" period of the fly's passage across the glare. How often the best fish of the day is lost at the moment of the angler's blindness!

Furthermore, when the angler faces the light, he makes the surface impenetrable to sight. Fish activity under water at any distance becomes wholly invisible. Nymph fishing thus loses one of its most favourable circumstances. On the other hand, at early dawn or late evening, facing the light can give the angler one of his most enjoyable experiences, a mysterious view of a watery world into which he cannot see but from which comes unexpected excitement. And he may prefer the suddennesses of fishing against the light even at the cost of some success.

Polarising glasses, of course, will mitigate the inconvenience. They save eyestrain by removing much of the reflected glare. But they also reduce the total amount of light available for vision.

Now consider the trout's view. It doesn't enjoy bright light in its eyes any more than the angler. Having no eyelids it can neither blink nor peer. When the sun is high and bright it illumines the bottom and the trout naturally looks in the direction of easier vision or else "sleeps", with its attention switched off until something stimulating excites it again.

In these bright midday conditions the trout frequently shows a comparative lack of skill in intercepting surface food; it misses or rises short. It, too, has blind spots caused by the light in its eyes; whereas at the beginning or end of the day, when the slanting light is weakened, the trout can take things from the surface with maximum precision when they come within its field of special attention.

On cloudy days, when the light is evenly filtered and seems to come from no particular direction, the trout's attention is less specialised. Any object coming towards it, either on its left or its right, will command its active interest. But when the light has a definite point of origin, the trout will direct its attention down-light rather than the other way.

One eye will be shielded from the direct rays, and objects in its field of attention will be brightly illuminated, including the

angler and his polished rod, which will heliograph warnings
straight to the eye of the fish. The trout's other eye, looking
up-light, will be much less efficient. Objects in its field (comparatively, a field of *inattention*) will appear in silhouette or merged
into the darker background.

This theory of the trout's contrasting fields of attention and
inattention in conditions of slanting light is surely a reasonable
one. Attention is a normal brain function in the process of
perception. The trout, with its unshielded eyes, has special need
of such means of avoiding the effects of glare. Not that this is its
only protection.

The trout's eyes are constantly bathed in cool water and need
no saving tears. Water is less transparent to light than air and
the trout can increase its protection against glare by sinking
deeper—but only at the expense of discrimination since it is a
short-sighted creature. In shallow water, or when it chooses to
swim high and near the surface, the trout is less handicapped by
short sight. In fact, in these circumstances, when its field of
attention is most specialised, it can see movements as far off as
twenty or even thirty yards. Surely, therefore, it would be wiser
for the angler to choose to position himself in the field of the
trout's inattention rather than the other; that is, to fish with the
light coming from behind him and towards the trout.

To do this, which is in contradiction of the simple rule of
thumb usually advocated, has one special advantage. It gives the
angler his best vision *into* the water. At the distance of his flies he
may be able to observe the take or detect what Skues taught us to
look for when nymphing, "the little brown wink under-water".

Nevertheless, it must be admitted that fishing down the light
has its special disadvantage. It throws the angler's shadow in
front of him over the water he desires to fish. I maintain, however,
that this difficulty is rather an exaggerated one and need not
handicap the angler if he is fully aware of it and acts suitably.
He can minimise the handicap in several ways—by taking
advantage of high banks, bushes, or trees in whose greater
shadows his own may be swallowed. He can reduce the length of
his shadow by keeping low or wading deep, by casting a longer
line than usual so as to reach beyond his shadow, or by horizontal
casting so as to avoid his rod shadow falling on the fishing area.

Some of these methods are not possible on narrow streams,

when the original simple rule of thumb may be the only resource. But there are other variations on this problem.

It seldom happens that the angler casts a shadow directly in line with his cast. Fortunately, it often falls at a pronounced angle to the flow of the stream, and if this angle is in the other quarter from that in which he wishes to fish then he has a larger sweep of water available. An angle of 45° in one direction will give him 90° or more in the other, with every possibility of success. He must move slowly all the time.

Trout are not frightened so much by the shadow *per se* as by its sudden appearance or movement. A slowly moving shadow will cause, at most, a nervous reaction in its own vicinity, but is unlikely to cause a spread of contagious fear, as happens when terrified fish flee into neighbouring areas.

I have often fished a pool successfully, my shadow slowly following the path of my flies as I proceeded downstream from cast to cast. Something similar is possible when upstream dry-fly fishing, except that the angle of shadow has to be in the other direction.

Apart from these tactics to avoid casting shadow, there are two others that have to do with the trout's fields of attention and inattention. They are especially important for the dry-fly fisher when he has marked down his fish or knows its probable lie.

It is a great advantage to present the fly in its field of attention. When the angler faces the light, this means he should drop the fly on the near side of the fish. This is a special recommendation for the rule of thumb, since the tactic then is fairly easy and the trout has every chance of seeing only the fly because it is near it: the nylon is further away and less likely to be noticed.

When the angler has the light behind him, ideally he should drop the fly on the far side of the fish, because that is its field of attention. Of course, there is a real danger of lining the fish and, in this case, the advanced angler's technique of the shepherd's crook cast, which brings the fly to the fish ahead of the nylon, is the supreme tactic.

Finally, let me reassure beginners, or those who think my suggestions are only for the very skilful, that the ideal is not necessary for successful fishing down-light. Wind and current often co-operate by providing a broken surface to the water. Not only do ripples and current help to obscure the attachments, but they also break up shadows; another reason why we should not be bound to the simple rule of thumb.

Nevertheless, the rule of thumb is a good one not to be lightly ignored. There is no good argument for deliberately projecting one's shadow over the fish. An experienced fisherman is always aware of the position of the sun or the moon and his normal preference will be to face the main source of light. This, however, is not always possible and occasionally he bends the rule for special purposes; but never carelessly or without extreme care to obviate the real dangers of so doing.

[15]

Drifting the Dry Fly Down

I wish I were in Lapland, to buy a good wind of one of the honest Witches,
that sell so many winds there, and so cheap.   IZAAK WALTON

There is no question about the principle of up or up-and-across
casting of the dry fly; though sometimes and in some places it has
to be modified to suit particular circumstances. Two special
difficulties that may demand such modifications are drag and
adverse wind. On fast-flowing rivers, such as the Derbyshire Wye,
a method of casting the fly downstream is sometimes adopted to
avoid drag. It is a rather clumsy resort, not always successful.
The angler has to pull the cast back so that the fly alights higher
up than the length of the cast would determine. Thereafter, the
fly precedes the leader and line as the slack is straightened out by
the current. The presentation thus made is ideal for two reasons:
the trout is not lined and drag is eliminated; but awkward for
another two: the slack line offers no resistance to the strike and
tends to pull the hook out of the trout's open mouth. All the
same, it is occasionally a very useful item in the repertoire of
dry-fly tactics. I have occasionally seen the same result accomplished by the use of a bubble float to carry the fly downstream
in places where ordinary casting is impossible, as where the river
flows through an avenue of overhanging trees, a method of fly
fishing which resembles trotting the worm for grayling. Many
fisheries, perhaps rightly, forbid the bubble float. In any case it
is not likely to be required on well-managed fisheries where
overgrown banks are not commonly tolerated.

Downstream drifting, without the awkwardness of the pulled
cast or the use of a bubble float, may be practised with considerable success on certain rivers which are exposed to strong
downstream winds. I illustrate this tactic by reference to my own

experiences on one such river. Similar methods will be possible, perhaps necessary, on many others in various parts of the country.

The waters of the upper Clyde can give memorable fishing to the hardy and resourceful angler. From Elvanfoot upwards to Watermeetings, where Daer and Potrail become the titular stream, the character of the river and its high, exposed situation present special problems. The main direction of the stream is northwards, as if driven by the ever-strong prevailing wind. But it flows with slow silent power, winding in great loops through a bleak inhospitable moor. Occasional shallow runs or narrow headlong rushes separate the long deep flats, but more often one flat leads almost imperceptibly into another. They are by no means easy to fish even at the best of times. Trotting a float as for grayling (and grayling are quite numerous) is the simplest technique, but most anglers practise the traditional downstream wet fly, which would be more successful in the varied lower reaches from Elvanfoot down to Thankerton. On favourable occasions, when the wind is upstream or not too strong, dry fly or nymph fishing is best of all.

But these opportunities are rare. All too often the wind sweeps unremittingly and fiercely downstream. Then casting against it is quite impossible, and most anglers abandon any preference for the dry fly. But this is not so much wisdom as capitulation. It is not necessary to surrender to the wind. If you can't beat it, join it. The dry fly can still prove the most successful method, if the angler will just come to terms with the wind. This part of upper Clyde is ideal for drifting a floating fly downstream, a method of fishing that has its own special skills and satisfactions.

In the flood plain below Watermeetings the banks are not too high for crawling nor too far apart for fishing the fly as near the opposite side as may be necessary. If you want to be quite inconspicuous it is almost everywhere possible to wade about knee-deep close to the nearside bank. With the wind behind you it is seldom difficult to stretch a medium cast downstream at 45°; the smoother the water the longer the cast and the smaller the angle to the stream. In my experience the best fish lie close to the sandy banks, except sometimes when hatching duns induce them to leave their holts and rove. The most productive technique is to drop the fly within two or three inches of the bank, within the narrow band of olive shadow or reflection which the bank casts on the stream. Here the fly is easily distinguishable as it floats down following the contour of the bank. If it falls short of the shadowed fringe of water, or drifts out of it, it becomes much more difficult to keep in sight, especially if it is light coloured, for the surface elsewhere reflects the sky and is grey or silvery, and, in sunshine, stippled with light. Although the surface is disturbed by the wind (a favourable circumstance), the current is normally slow and even, so that there is little trouble with drag. By careful crawling or wading, it is often possible to follow the progress of the fly at an even distance for as much as twenty or thirty yards before it becomes necessary to renew the cast. Of course, the line is a floater or made to float. The nylon also may be greased up to about a foot from the fly. A take is seldom conspicuous. The sudden disappearance of the fly may be the only indication. Any break on the surface is immediately obliterated unless in a very sheltered corner where the wind has less effect. So it pays to keep alert.

One can often anticipate the moment of a take. As you follow the fly, some slight disturbance ahead of it, perhaps no more than a hump on the surface or a bursting bubble, will betray a feeding fish, and a moment later your fly will be added to the menu. You should be ready for it. Anticipation, however, is more a matter of reading the contour of the bank than the surface of the water. Wherever there is a break in the sandy wall, such as a tiny bay or the mouth of a spring, wherever an old, flood-captured fence-post or a tuft of rushes projects into the stream, causing some alteration in the flow, these are places where trout may be expected. Undercut banking, ready to fall, or lumps of grassy bank already fallen, provide shelter for fish and variations in the current. Don't expect very big catches. One or two trout from each flat is good going. But they are likely to be considerable fish, very active and anything from half pound up to an occasional three times that weight.

Surprisingly, you will discover that upstream casting is sometimes possible because of the meandering of the stream. There is one very productive flat a short distance below the mouth of the Potrail which makes a great ox-bow bend midway. You have to float the fly down to the bend where casting becomes more difficult and the water very choppy because, under the influence of the wind, it is trying to go in two opposite directions at once. Then you cross over the peninsula to begin again at the bottom of the next flat and fish up to the bend where you broke off. I usually fish this second part very slowly and then go back and repeat the process because I enjoy the chance of fishing the dry fly in normal fashion; that is, upstream with wind in my favour. Besides, it's a very fishy stretch of water.

The same technique of drifting the fly downstream with a strong following wind may be practised with a nymph or a combination of nymph and dry fly, the floating dropper acting as a float or indicator. However, I usually find the dry fly quite successful enough. The water is seldom so deep that nymph-feeding trout will fail to notice a floater.

Although I first learned to drift the dry fly downstream out of necessity on the contrary upper Clyde, which I still regard as ideally suited to the method, I have often found it serviceable on other waters under similar conditions. If, like me, you hanker after the delights of dry-fly fishing and prefer to practise it somehow, at least some of the time in spite of seemingly un-favourable circumstances, you will add to your pleasure by settling with the adverse wind instead of struggling against it. Float your fly down the water towards the waiting trout.

PART V

Flies of the River

[16]

Fly Selection

HAMLET: *Dost know this water-fly?*   WILLIAM SHAKESPEARE

The problems of fly selection, not unknown to Shakespeare, are with us still. Every Hamlet asks the same questions at the water-side: What are they taking? What fly is that? Even when these get some sort of answers, he still suffers from doubt and indecision: What artificial shall I use?

Such difficulties should at last be easier to resolve. The scientist has pretty well established his insect classifications. Angling writers today are disagreeing less about the names they use for identified insects. But there is a historical back-log. Older writers, local traditions, and the tackle trade tend to perpetuate names that are strictly out of date. The confusion is greater in regard to artificial representations. Fly-tyers have exercised ingenuity, vanity, and sense of humour in their choice of names. Thousands of creations are described and may be available, named from the materials of their construction—Waterhen Bloa, Partridge and Yellow; or named after their inventors—Greenwell's Glory, Lunn's Particular; or named just for the fun of it—Tup's Indispensable, Bloody Butcher.

There is no specific answer for all occasions; but a simple conspectus of fly identification is possible, such as will enable a fisherman to start confidently and have a fair measure of success therefore. The Confidence Fly, whatever its other names, is still the best at the end of his line, and, as they say on the Clyde: "It's the flee on the watter that catches the troot." There is plenty of scope left for further study, for the subject is a considerable one which will outlast a lifetime. When Hamlet goes fishing, doubt and indecision need no longer cripple his mind.

There are several ways in which he can assist himself besides using the conspectus. There is no harm in asking other anglers what they are using or finding successful. The best answers are the names of natural flies—olives, pale wateries, etc. Natural flies are much less numerous than artificials and the conspectus is based on them. But to be told about a Greenwell or Hare's Ear is almost as valuable, for these are general patterns in the conspectus. Occasionally answers may be of little or no value and he is left to his own devices.

One of these is a practical study of entomology. The fisherman should endeavour to identify the natural insect by three principal methods—observation, capture, autopsy. Just to watch flies as they float down the stream may give a fair idea of what they are. Size and colour are recognisable clues. A little flat muslin net, attached to your rod, or just your hat, would enable you to catch one or two specimens. This makes positive identification more certain or, failing that, a more confident selection from the contents of the fly box.

Autopsies may be of two kinds. You can empty out the stomach contents of your catch when you get home and thus discover what they were feeding on some hours ago. Digestion, which continues after death, may rather spoil this method. A long-handled marrow spoon, first recommended by G E M Skues, can be used as soon as a fish has been killed. Inserted down the gullet and turned, it will extract the contents. If these are put into a shallow white dish of water, it is possible to discover what the fish has just been feeding on. Marrow spoons now command antique prices: a cut-bowl, long-handled teaspoon will do just as well, or a piece of plastic tubing, cut to half-section at one end. By such means the fisherman may greatly relieve his anxieties about fly identification and provide himself with an interesting and relevant hobby.

No originality is claimed for the list and conspectus that follows. They are based on a series of natural flies that succeed one another through the season on most running waters. These are matched with recommended artificials, according to stages of development in the natural insects—nymph, hatching nymph, wet fly, dun, spinner. The fisherman may choose whatever artificial suits the fly he has identified or expects to find from the information given. He may begin by making up a spring cast, or a summer one, leaving more positive identifications until he has acquired experience. Whichever method he adopts he should proceed confidently from that point on. Confidence and persistence will bring rewards: whereas doubt and indecision spell failure.

It will be noted that general, or standard, patterns—Greenwell, Hare's Ear, Pheasant Tail Spinner—recur frequently, each representing several insects. It would be possible to fish with one or more of these throughout the season and be quite sure of considerable success. Variations in hook size and shade would still be necessary: flies in the olive series, for instance, decrease in size and become paler in colour as the season proceeds. Many well-known experts specialise in this way. All the same I would recommend a fisherman not to stick at this stage of experience. He will enjoy adding to his repertoire and experimenting along the way.

The list and conspectus are limited in range, intended only as an introduction to fly selection. There are now available a number of excellent comprehensive books on the subject. A more serious limitation is that only the names of artificials and, sometimes, the names of their creators, are given. It is assumed that the fisherman using it does not yet tie his own flies and will purchase his requirements. Alternatives are given in many cases, so that if he cannot get one he may get another. In some cases I would recommend ordering by post from specialist fly tyers who advertise in the angling press, or getting in touch with a local fly-tying expert. There is usually one in each area who has acquired a reputation among anglers. Best of all, and the sooner the bettter, he should learn to tie his own flies. "No direction can be given", said Izaak Walton, "to make a man of dull capacity able to make a flie well": but no such man could acquire any of the other skills of angling. Simple hackle flies are easy to master and quite satisfactory for all styles of fishing. To provide recipes for all the artificials given in the conspectus would take us beyond the scope of this book: but recommendations given in the book-list will be helpful when the fisherman is ready for further information.

I

LIST OF THE COMMONER DAY FLIES

Large Dark Olive (*Baëtis rhodani*)

OTHER FISHERMAN'S NAMES: Large Spring Olive, Blue Dun.

DESCRIPTION: Medium large. Dark olive-grey body. Smoky wings. Two tails.

SEASON: Early spring and late autumn.

HOOK SIZE: 14.

NYMPH: Dark Greenwell (Lawrie), Olive Nymph (Sawyer), P V C Nymph (Goddard).

HATCHING NYMPH: Gold Ribbed Hare's Ear.

WET FLY: Dark Greenwell, Waterhen Bloa, Orange Grouse.

DUN: Olive Quill, dark Greenwell, Imperial (Kite).

SPINNER: Pheasant Tail, Large Red Spinner, Lunn's Particular.

NOTES: Spinner is seldom seen on the water, perhaps because it arrives there after dark.

Iron Blue (*Baëtis pumilus or niger*)

DESCRIPTION: Small. Very dark brown-olive body. Dull grey-blue wings: looks black from distance. Two tails.

SEASON: May, early June, September, October.

HOOK SIZE: 15, 16.

NYMPH: I B D Nymph (Skues, Lawrie), dark Greenwell.

HATCHING NYMPH: I B D Hatching Nymph (Lawrie).

WET FLY: Dark Watchet, Snipe and Purple. I B D (Skues).

DUN: I B Quill, Imperial, Hawthorn.

SPINNER: Houghton Ruby, Lunn's Particular, Pheasant Tail, Claret Spinner.

NOTES: Good in adverse weather conditions. Spent spinners may be taken at any time of day, usually in or under the surface film. Skues's dressing of wet fly or nymph, dressed with short sparse soft feathers from the jackdaw's throat, is a good fly. It may be fished dry if it can be kept afloat.

March Brown (*Rhithrogena haarupi*)

DESCRIPTION: Large. Body brown, tinged with reddish brown. Brown-mottled fawn wings. Two tails.

SEASON: Late March to early May. Another form in autumn.

HOOK SIZE: 12.

NYMPH AND WET FLY: Partridge and Orange, Gold M B, etc.

HATCHING NYMPH: (Lawrie).
DUN: Partridge and Orange, etc.
SPINNER: Great Red Spinner, Pheasant Tail, etc.
NOTES: Commonest in north and west rough rivers. Rises tend to
be prolific but of short duration, one or more following at
intervals in rough water. The hatching nymph is most successful.

March Brown is a good taking fly outside its own season:
perhaps taken for shrimp. There is an autumn form of it.

Medium Olive (*Baëtis vernus*, or *tenax*, or *buceratus*)

OTHER NAME: Yellow Dun.
DESCRIPTION: Medium size. Pale brown-olive body. Dull grey
wings. Two tails.
SEASON: Throughout season from mid-May.
HOOK SIZE: 15.
NYMPH: Light Greenwell, Medium Olive Nymph (Skues).
HATCHING NYMPH: Light G R H E.
WET FLY: Light Greenwell, Olive Upright.
DUN: Blue Dun, Olive Quill, Dogsbody, Greenwell.
SPINNER: Pheasant Tail, Tup's Indispensable, Lunn's Particular,
Red Quill, Red Spinner.

Small Dark Olive (*Baëtis scambus*)

OTHER FISHERMAN'S NAMES: July Dun, Pale Watery.
DESCRIPTION: Small or very small. Grey-olive body. Darkish
grey wings. Two tails. Smaller edition of Large Dark Olive.
SEASON: July, August.
HOOK SIZE: 15 or 16.
NYMPH: Olive Nymph (Sawyer), PVC Nymph (Goddard), dark
Greenwell.
HATCHING NYMPH: G R H E.
WET FLY: Small dark Greenwell, Poult Bloa, Snipe Bloa, Blue
Upright.
DUN: Yellow Halo (Goddard), July Dun.
SPINNER: Pheasant Tail, small Red Spinner, Lunn's Particular.
NOTES: Less common in Scotland and Ireland. Comes on before
noon and may continue till tea-time. Towards end of June
may appear in late evening.

Pale Watery (*Baëtis bioculatus*)

DESCRIPTION: Small. Pale grey-olive body shading to yellow-olive near tail. Pale grey wings. Two tails.

SEASON: Late May to October.

HOOK SIZE: 15, 16.

NYMPH: Pale Watery Nymph (Sawyer or Lawrie), light Greenwell.

HATCHING NYMPH: (Lawrie).

WET FLY: Tup, Partridge and Yellow, Ginger Quill.

DUN: Blue Quill, Little Marryat (Skues), Yellow Halo (Goddard), Last Hope (Goddard), Tup, Lock's Fancy, Ginger Quill.

SPINNER: Tup, Lunn's Yellow Boy, P W Spinner, Golden Spinner.

NOTES: Southern England, chalk streams.

Three other olives have been known as Pale Wateries. The name should be reserved for this fly.

Blue Winged Olive (*Ephemerella ignita*)

DESCRIPTION: Medium large. Bright green body, darkening to rusty brown towards end of season. Dark blue-grey wings. Three tails.

SEASON: Mid-June onwards.

HOOK SIZE: 14.

NYMPH: Medium Olive Nymph (Skues), light Greenwell.

HATCHING NYMPH: G R H E, Lunn's Hackle Blue Wing.

WET FLY: G R H E, Poult Bloa, Grouse and Orange.

DUN: Orange Quill, B W O.

SPINNER: Sherry Spinner (Skues or Woolley), Port Spinner, Pheasant Tail.

NOTES: Perhaps commonest fly of all. Occurs on rivers of all kinds and large lakes. Spinner causes evening rise at dusk until August. Occurs on late afternoons thereafter.

Pale Evening Dun (*Procloëon pseudorufulum*)

DESCRIPTION: Medium size. Pale straw body. Pale grey wings. Two tails.

SEASON: Summer months, late in day.

HOOK SIZE: 15.

NYMPH: Spurwing/P W Nymph (Sawyer).

DUN: Pale Evening Dun (Kite).

NOTES: Hatches at dusk or late evening often along with B W O.
Slower flowing reaches of river.

Mayfly (*Ephemera danica or vulgata*)

OTHER NAMES: Green Drake, Spent Gnat.
DESCRIPTION: Very large. Greyish-white body, mottled brown.
Grey wings with dark markings. Three tails.
SEASON: Late May or early June for about two weeks.
HOOK SIZE: 9–12.
NYMPH: Veniard's three patterns.
HATCHING NYMPH: Mayfly Hatching Nymph (C F Walker).
WET FLY: Veniard's three patterns.
SPINNER: Spent Mayfly (Veniard), Nevamis Mayfly (Goddard),
Green Drake Upright (Jacques).
NOTES: Nymphs and wet flies should be used at beginning of rise,
half-submerged. Spinners thereafter. Mayfly less common
than it used to be.

Little Sky Blue (*Centroptilum luteolum*)

OTHER NAMES: Small or Lesser Spurwing, Pale Watery.
DESCRIPTION: Medium to small. Pale olive body. Very pale grey
wings. Two tails.
SEASON: Early May to September or October.
HOOK SIZE: 15, 16.
NYMPH: Pale Watery (Lawrie), Spurwing/P W Nymph (Sawyer).
HATCHING NYMPH: Pale Watery (Lawrie).
WET FLY: Tup, light Greenwell.
DUN: Pale Watery, Tup, Lock's Fancy.
SPINNER: Pheasant Tail, Lunn's Particular, Little Amber Spinner.
NOTES: Very common everywhere. All day in earlier part of
season, late afternoon and evening afterwards.

Sedge Flies

There are many species of sedge, or caddis, flies, some of
which are very important to the trout fisherman. They are most
useful towards the end of the summer, especially in the evening
and after dark. Trout will often accept a sedge representation
even when the natural fly is not on the water. As a rule they
are fished on the surface—drag, for once, being no disadvantage.
The natural fly may often be seen, after hatching, scarpering

across the water towards the shelter of the bank. I have had great pleasure tying Joscelyn Lane's Trimmed Hackle Sedges and used them to good effect: in his book he gives seven recipes. The following list may be available in the shops and is more orthodox than Lane's.

Grannom (*Brachycentrus subnubilis*)

OTHER NAME: Greentail.

SEASON: April–May.

DESCRIPTION: Green egg masses. Fawn-grey wings with dark markings.

HOOK SIZE: 14, 15.

REPRESENTATION: Grannom (Henry and Powell).

NOTES: Earliest Sedge. Day flying. Massive hatches from noon on. Fast water.

Great Red Sedge (*Phryganea grandis and striata*)

OTHER NAME: Murragh.

DESCRIPTION: Largest of the Sedges. Reddish-brown wings, mottled with lighter markings.

SEASON: May–July. Late evening.

HOOK SIZE: 8–12.

REPRESENTATIONS: Brown Sedge, large Alder, John Storey.

Little Red Sedge (*Tinodes waeneri*)

DESCRIPTION: Small. Long, hairy, with yellow-brown wings.

SEASON: June onwards, evening.

HOOK SIZE: 14.

REPRESENTATIONS: Little Red Sedge (Skues), Invicta.

Cinnamon Sedge (*Limnephilus lunatus and others*)

DESCRIPTION: Medium size. Green or brownish body. Mottled or plain cinnamon wings.

SEASON: June onwards. Throughout day or early evening.

HOOK SIZE: 10–12.

REPRESENTATIONS: Cinnamon Sedge (Woolley), Invicta.

NOTES: *Limnephilus lunatus* has moon-shaped markings; nicknamed Loony Phyllis.

Caperer (*Halesus radiatus*)

DESCRIPTION: Large red or cinnamon wings. Orange body.
SEASON: August onwards, early or late evening.
HOOK SIZE: 12–14.
REPRESENTATION: Caperer (Lunn).
NOTE: Very common.

Conspectus of Flies

Natural Flies   *Artificials*

	Spring	Summer	Autumn
March Browns	*M B* (12) Partridge and Orange Great Red Spinner Pheasant Tail	—	*Late M B* (12) as spring
Olives and Pale Watery	L D O (14) dark Greenwell G R H E Imperial Pheasant Tail	M O (15) S D O (15, 16) P W (15, 16) B W O (14) Greenwell G R H E Tup Pheasant Tail	as summer — as summer as summer
Pale Evening Dun	—	*P E Dun* (15) P W Nymph (Sawyer) P E Dun (Kite)	—
Iron Blue	*I B* (15, 16) Dark Greenwell Snipe and Purple Claret Spinner Pheasant Tail	as spring (early June)	as spring

Conspectus of Flies

Natural Flies   *Artificials*

	Spring	Summer	Autumn
Sedges	*Grannom* (14, 15) Grannom *Great Red Sedge* (8–12) Brown Sedge John Storey	*Little Red Sedge* (14) Little Red Sedge (Skues) Invicta *Cinnamon Sedge* (10) Cinnamon Sedge (Woolley) Invicta	*Caperer* (12, 14) Caperer (Lunn)

[17]

Evening Rise

The look of the evening rise is so often the best of it.   EARL GREY

The duration of the evening rise is all too short, and the angler is always conscious of the approaching darkness when a phantom voice will cry "Time, gentlemen, please!"   C F WALKER

In the following three chapters I propose to discuss taking times, when trout are likely to be most active. I have no special theories about these. My own actual experience is almost always confirmed by that of my predecessors whom, therefore, it is a pleasure to quote. I am inclined to be sceptical about attempts to reduce this subject to over-simple terms. It is likely to remain a matter of animal behaviour in response to such a variety of circumstances as to defeat precision and prophecy. I expose myself, therefore, to the risk of being proved obtuse when I say that nothing in my experience has so far confirmed the sol-lunar theory. This ascribes taking times to the tidal influence of the moon on even small waters like rivers and lakes. It is claimed that they can be determined accurately on the calendar and fully relied upon, provided suitable allowances are made for less general influences such as local weather conditions. If true, this theory could revolutionise our knowledge of the times of the take and remove much of the uncertainty we feel about the prospects of our fishing expeditions. I remain unconvinced and can say nothing comparably precise on the subject. The sport of fishing seems to be characterised by uncertainty and I, like most other fishermen, seem to prefer it so.

I propose, first, to give separate consideration to the evening rise and the overnight taking times, as these are "special", and in the third chapter deal with the rest of the day.

Trout, like all earth's creatures, live for twenty-four hours of the day. Since, as we have discovered, they seek their food almost exclusively by use of their eyesight, it is reasonable to suppose that their feeding is limited to the daylight hours. This, for the most part, is true. In the half-light of midsummer nights, and also later in the season when warm moist weather brings out sedges and moths, and moonlight helps the trout to see them, activity may continue from dusk to dawn: but for the rest of the year daylight measures their feeding times.

There is evidence that trout's vision is especially acute at the extremes of day when slanting light reveals objects by side illumination, or silhouettes them against an illuminated background.

In the evening the intensity of the light is diminished, since it is filtered through a vastly increased depth of atmosphere. Similar conditions pertain earlier in the day whenever the sky is obscured by a pall of high cloud so that the light is evenly filtered and seems not to come from any definite direction. At such times trout are capable of very precise discrimination of the form and colour of objects in or on the water. These are good conditions for fishing, though the angler has to exercise all his skill "to display the insignificant and conceal the obvious". The late evening is notorious for the maddening selectivity that accompanies the trout's feeding excitement.

To miss out on these occasions, therefore, which is what many anglers do, is surely unfortunate, to say the least. Those who have to travel long distances for their sport, or conform to bus or train timetables, may have no option. But the private motor car provides for a much more elastic day. Yet I see little evidence of changes in fishing habits, which makes me wonder if fishers are affected by a sort of industrial hangover. Most of them seem to believe in an eight-hour day—even for fishing, which is absurd. The fish don't.

An evening rise can occur at any part of the season, though it acquires the definite article only in midsummer. I remember one that came on at half-past six on the opening day, appropriately the first of April. It was a humiliating experience. Another happened in May and was timed by the chimes of Peebles town clock as it struck seven o'clock and the quarters before and after. As the chimes of 7.15 died away I was making my final casts, prolonged prayers that were ignored by the cavorting trout. Then I had to run for my train. Experiences such as these make angling a branch of philosophy.

It is a surprising fact that latitude, even in Britain which extends north and south, has little or no effect on the habits and growth of trout; except, I suggest, in respect of the evening rise. Twilight lasts longer in the north: in fact, in Orkney and Shetland, it may last all night. This has affected the sensibilities of Scots, angler and non-angler alike. They have a larger share of the joys and anguish associated with the twilight; and the angler even more so, for he experiences extended evening rises.

Short evening rises, earlier or later in the season, may not be taken too seriously, accepted as bonus to a good day or as just a final test of character on a bad one. But from mid-June, through July and into August, the Tweedside angler specialises from dusk to dark. It is a challenging, and often profitable, test of skill.

The skill is a matter of observation and accumulated experience. In the half-light observation is difficult and experience (one's own or others') is more valuable. It concerns the flies on or in the water. If an evening rise comes on there are likely to be more of them than at any other time of day. The end of a pleasant, peaceful day is a favourite time for the hatching out of duns. Nymphs rise towards the surface and the trout begin to get busy making bulging rise forms. Presently, as the duns pop out and float on the stream, more distinctive bell-form rises may disturb the reflections of the sunset's afterglow: the double whorl or kidney shaped rise form which distinguishes the taking of the Blue Winged Olive may give even more definite indications to the watching angler. As the light fades the rises may become less conspicuous for that reason and for another, namely, that trout have begun to select spent spinners from the plentiful offerings on the water and are merely dimpling the surface as they cruise beneath, sipping as they go. Finally, as the light begins to leave the sky and the water turns silvery grey or mysteriously black (according to direction of view), splashing rises may commence again, indicating the taking of sedges as they scutter along the surface towards the safety of the bank. To cope with such successive and different phases of the evening rise is obviously a matter of considerable skill. There is no single easy solution.

Nymph fishing, especially at the start, would seem good advice: but detecting the take of a nymph, not easy at any time, is especially difficult in the diminishing light. Oliver Kite, whom few could rival in skill with the nymph, has written that he uses it during the evening rise only when he is fishing for challenges: for pleasure he prefers a dry fly, his own Imperial, for preference. I sometimes use a sunk nymph when the water is big, which is not a favourable condition for the evening rise, but fish it downstream so that takes register by feel. More often, like the majority, I fish a dry fly chosen on the basis of experience rather than as a result of observation.

There may be a variety of duns and spinners on the water. On some happy, perhaps rare, occasions the trout may be taking them at random. Any one of several possible flies may then prove successful—Medium Olive, Pale Watery, B W O. More often, it seems, even when there is a multiple choice, trout will feed selectively and the angler will have no luck with anything but the right fly. The trout may be specialising on nymphs, or duns, or spinners, of a particular species. To be sure of that species is never easy. The rise form, as already mentioned, may be a useful clue. Sometimes by close observation, or by intelligent trial and error, the fisherman may solve this problem early enough for success before the rise peters out: but changes of fly are time consuming and the ghostly voice that calls the end of the session may be heard before the fisherman has hit on the right solution. A further complication is when trout change from one fly to another in the course of the rise. This is likely to happen at least once when they transfer from small fly to sedge, usually as darkness approaches; but on some evenings it affects their choice among the smaller flies themselves. A fairly obvious tactic to meet these circumstances is to mount more than one fly on the leader. The evening rise is one of the times when I like to use two flies: these may be nymph on the tail and dun in the dropper position. Other alternatives are two dry flies, different species of dun or spinner. Because of the enormous numbers of flies on the water it may even pay to mount two dry flies of a single species in order to double the odds in favour of either being noticed by a trout. A regular feature of the evening rise is the large numbers of flies that are not taken even when the surface is boiling. The chances of any one fly being seen and taken are sometimes quite small. It is a matter of elementary observation that an evening rise on a loch sets the feeding trout roving along beneath the surface. There is good reason for thinking that river-trout on this occasion sometimes act similarly: for very often, when one casts over a rise form, nothing happens—perhaps because the trout that made it is no longer there. Even in a strong stream, as well as in the lower and quieter areas of a pool, trout will rove from place to place, selecting at each move whatever they fancy of what appears in their window. Two flies may help the fisherman in such circumstances.

Over the years a fisherman will try out a succession of tactics to defeat the evening rise. Naturally he believes most strongly in those that seem to have succeeded best—and, equally, in the latest of the series which may (and that is always the hope) eclipse all others. G E M Skues must be given the credit for a widespread faith, which I share, in the virtue of the Orange Quill. This dun representation has inspired a lot of talk. It bears no obvious resemblance to the dun of the B W O for which it is seemingly taken by the trout.

The practical angler will not be inhibited from using it on that score: that it succeeds in a most difficult situation is enough for him.

Another tip we owe to Skues is that trout will often take a spinner even when it is still feeding on the dun. The evening rise is a time to remember this one. The stage of the rise when duns are being taken is often too short for convenience. Furthermore, as soon as the fish begin on spinners, dun representations become quite useless. I often put up one or two spinners from the start, thus ignoring the nymph stage, and hoping to get credit at the brief dun as well as at the longer spinner stages of the rise. Let me quote here a couple of authoritative remarks by Skues which contain more wisdom, I believe, than I have found anywhere else:

"A Red Spinner during a rise of olives, a Claret Spinner when the iron blue is on, and a Sherry Spinner when the blue winged olive is on." This last, of course, has special reference to the subject of this chapter.

"If the angler is provided with Orange Quills . . . he may count on sport worth remembering, though possibly, not a spinner may be on the water at the time."

Sedge flies may come on at any time of the evening and the fisherman should be on the lookout for them. A Little Red Sedge is a valuable fly, even when the naturals have not yet appeared. At the end of the evening rise, when trout sometimes begin to splash about again, the Great Red Sedge or some form of Cinnamon Sedge, may be tried. I think the exact variety is not critical: almost any large representation, fished dry, is likely to succeed in favourable circumstances. It is important that the fisherman has a leader of one or two sedges, readily got at in the dark and easily attached to the reel line. It should be of stronger nylon, perhaps 7 lb breaking strain, to suit the larger flies and the heavier trout that may have to be managed in the growing dark. This is the one purpose for which I still use the loop and jam-knot method of attachment. Its clumsiness is less of a handicap: whereas a blood knot is a slower and sometimes very difficult knot to tie in the fading light.

Much more could be said about the evening rise: for example, the conditions that favour it. These apply equally to night fishing and may, therefore, be taken up in the discussion of that subject which follows in the next chapter.

[18]

Night Fishing

In the night the best Trouts come out of their holes. IZAAK WALTON

Night fishing is practised more by local fishermen than by visitors from a distance. The locals, like the trout, are sensitively adjusted to the conditions of the season, and practise a natural economy of effort. Even if they mistake the night and find the trout unresponsive, they lose no more than an hour or two, returning home without difficulty and with little loss of face. But anyone who has to make a distant expedition every time he goes fishing will think twice before he sets out for a night of it, especially if he has had a previous disappointment. He may be inclined to the view that night fishing is not all it's cracked up to be, which no doubt is true enough of any part of the sport of fishing and should be resisted. Night fishing can be the salvation of the summer holiday angler, which is where I came into it for the first time.

It was the last day of my holiday. Three trout in six days of brilliant July weather: I was learning the hard way that trout are not very interested in day flies at that time of year. Determined to get something to take home, I arrived at the river on the early side of 6 a m, the sun already hot even then, everything calm, bright, and hopeless. At the first pool I came on the prostrate body of a man, a fisher, in waders. His rod speared to the turf. His basket, a large one, lay open beside him where he had carelessly let it drop. He was fast asleep.

Then I saw the contents of his basket. It was full to the brim of enormous trout. I understood at once. Here was that fabulous creature, a night fisher.

That vision splendid converted me for ever. I too would join the mystery, practise the mystique of the big fly. Not that year;

but there have been too many others since. I no longer grieve for the tapering off of the spring fishing. During the dog-days I choose a suitable evening and am off, in a quiet excitement of mind, to explore the other world of night. Brownies, grayling, or the nerve shattering sea-trout—occasionally all three—have made the small hours memorable. I have never equalled the catch that converted me: and, if I see the dawn come in, that's usually when the night has been pleasant, promising, but ungenerous. Other times I am content with a modest reward for a few hours out of bed, where I usually finish the night.

The pleasures of this thing? Sometimes they are terrors, modified by familiarity, for the night has to be learnt: the cow that looms as large as an elephant; a bronchitic sheep that coughs just behind where you are casting; furtive rustling in the under-brush, which a torch reveals to be only a restless hedgehog.

You'd rather stay in bed? Then your nerves will never be plucked by the big fish that wait for the cover of night. Even if they often shrink in size and splendour under the baneful influence of daylight, they do something to you in the dark that you'll never forget.

Sometimes they take with a whiz, sometimes after a quiet fumbling which you thought was the drag of the moss on the stones. Sometimes they don't take, or only after long, patient waiting. The night is a considerable time, even in midsummer. Weather and the moods of fish may change several times, just as in daytime.

How does one choose a suitable night? If possible, get a local report, by telephone for instance, whenever the weather and water conditions have settled into a succession of favourable evenings. Or else, just use your own judgement of the circum-stances likely to obtain. Not too dogmatically, I suggest the following hopeful conditions: low water and warm, muggy air. When the margins of the river are clear and shallow trout rove about on suitable nights in search of food. Brimming banks after a lot of rain are bad conditions. Moths in your face, very promising. If the bats are flittering, good; but, if they soon dis-appear, that's a bad sign. Avoid clear nights after blazing cloud-less days. When the stars burn holes in the top of your head and all the heat goes up into space, the river tries to go up there, too. That's when it fills the air with a smoking mist which completely spoils fishing both at the evening rise time and for the rest of the night as long as it persists. Choose a darkish night with a gentle rain. A really wet night may also be good, provided it is not accompanied by strong wind which increases the angler's physical difficulties and seems to inhibit the take as well. A moon of any size, provided it plays hide and seek among the clouds, and rises or sets on the other side of the river, is a friendly companion during a long night's fishing, though some anglers don't share my approval of it. Certainly, when it hangs behind you it is more dangerous than the sun. C F Walker alleges that even the pallid daytime moon in that position is absolutely fatal to successful fishing; but up to the present I seem to have overlooked that ingenious excuse for a poor catch.

Undoubtedly the best of all auspices for a successful night-fishing expedition is a preceding good evening rise. The fisher who has taken a catch with small fly before ten o'clock will take more with the big fly after eleven. To him that hath. . . . Many of my best nights have not been planned: they have been extensions of afternoon or evening expeditions. In midsummer the angler is well advised to postpone his arrival at the waterside until most of the day is over and be prepared to stay till sundown for the sake of a possible evening rise. If this materialises, then he should stay on into the darkness for an hour or two, or longer, according to results, to experience the special pleasures that belong to fishing at night when trout are on the feed.

In the last chapter it was noted that the final phase of the evening rise in midsummer is usually when the sedges appear. As long as the light permits rises to be seen it is possible to fish floating representations of these: and even when it becomes difficult to see what happens on the surface, since sedges may be dragged, takes may be detected by feel. Often, however, a time comes when wet-fly fishing becomes more productive than dry. This may apply to the small fly as well as the big fly of night.

When the night is not dark, when the trout have a light sky as background to their window, they often continue to take small flies long after the usual termination of the evening rise, especially, perhaps, in the north where twilight is more prolonged. On such a night the large sedges may postpone their appearance. Scottish anglers frequently change their tactics in the latter part of the evening rise. They remove the dry fly from the end

K

of their leader and substitute a wet fly, a favourite one being a light Partridge and Yellow, which they now fish downstream for as long as the trout continue to take an interest in it. Unless a very brilliant moon makes upstream dry fly possible again at some later period, they will continue to fish wet fly for the rest of the night, changing over to larger representations as soon as the trout or the sedges give the word, which they usually do within the hour.

Those who are disinclined to remain out of bed tend to rationalise their condemnation of night fishing. They allege the occasional experience of big or multiple catches as the norm and cry bad sport. There may be good reason on some fisheries for limiting or even forbidding night fishing. On some of the waters I fish the rule is one hour after sundown: but I am happy on others to have the opportunity to fish at night. I have never had anything like a phenomenal catch. Night fishing gives one the hope of events out of the ordinary: such as the taking of a large fish that would not likely rise to fly during the daylight hours. The thing is possible and, added to the other unusual experiences of fishing in the dark, gives another dimension to the pleasures of angling.

No special equipment is necessary. It is important to put on a stronger leader than would be appropriate by day. This is to suit the larger flies and the larger fish that may be taken, but more especially to make the actual fishing easier. Tangles are very frustrating at night and occur more frequently in thin nylon. A spare leader easily accessible (wrapped round your hat, for instance) saves a lot of fumbling. It should be about 7 lb breaking strain at the point.

The flies are any of the larger night-flying sedges which are best fished dry at the earlier period of the night. They may be very bushy specimens. Later on it is usual to use more streamlined large wet flies. They may still resemble the sedges in colouration, but also tinsel bodied sea-trout or loch flies will prove suitable. When fish are seen or heard to be making forays among the minnows in the shallow margins, fish-fry lures, which are popular with loch fishers, may prove very successful on the river. Where the rules permit, it is common practice to tip the fly with a maggot, and on some nights this greatly increases the chances of a take. Whether this is fly or bait fishing is open to question. To avoid handling such bait and to retain fly-fishing status, some anglers substitute a small piece of white leather for the maggot: but whether this is effective or not I cannot say. It is best to limit the number of flies on the leader. One is sufficient: any more than two is asking for trouble rather than trout; though I have seen Clydeside anglers expertly managing anything up to five or six.

Wading at night is obviously a much more dangerous proceeding than it is by day. If the water is low, as is most desirable, there is less danger as well as less occasion for it. If wading is necessary, it should only be done in familiar circumstances. Even after a daylight reconnaissance the angler may find the night-shrouded river a very bewildering place. He should never wade where he has not waded previously. The hole or the rock which he successfully avoided in daylight is a very different proposition at night. Plunging about, moreover, is no less frightening to the fish.

In any case, wading is less necessary. The trout tend to move about at night. The fisherman should choose a suitable pool before darkness sets in: one with a strand of gravel alongside the main stream, down which he can move quietly and safely as he explores it. He may thus spend the whole night in one main area, much of the time without any change of stance at all, depending on the roving trout to come within range.

It is possible to improve your night vision by a diet of carrots: but you'll still need a torch to help with the inevitable tangle or occasional change of fly. I am always most careful to avoid shining it on the water, though I rather like the illumination of car headlights when they sweep across the stream as the traffic rounds a bend in the road: so I am more cautious than consistent in my thinking about this. Sometimes it is necessary to use the torch at the moment of netting a trout: but it is remarkable how dark-adapted one's eyes become and things which seem impossible in theory become quite easy in practice, because midsummer nights are seldom wholly dark, except in the shade of trees or high banks.

Having now dealt with the evening rise and the practice of night fishing we can proceed to a consideration of the total period of the twenty-four hours with a view to ascertaining the most likely times of the take.

[19]

Times of the Take

The time of the take . . . occurs at some time of the day the whole season through.
W C STEWART

If you want to get the most out of your fishing, I suggest you make the most of every day. If that means an occasional ordeal, what about it? Ordeals are good for the young. But fishing by ordeal is not really necessary. You can fish throughout the twenty-four hour cycle and enjoy every minute of it, if you spread it over the season. That simple solution is too seldom practised. Many good fishing hours are lost. Anglers limit, thereby, their experience, their catches, and their pleasure.

The "time of the take" is the essence of the matter. If the angler knows it and is ready for it, success is at least possible, and, given some skill, almost certain. Chance plays a part. If an angler keeps at it long enough he is likely to meet with the take sooner or later. But its onset may find him weary and jaded, unable to make the best of his opportunity. Worse still, he may be eating his lunch. To avoid fasting I recommend staggered meal times for anglers and fish.

Reading the literature is a pleasure and a help. Thereby, the angler gets a theoretical expectation of certain special taking times, such as the noonday and evening rises, but he should be warned—many angling writers, especially the modern ones, tend also to suffer from industrial hangover. There is no real substitute for practical first-hand experience of every hour of the twenty-four, and this is to be recommended to beginners, especially the young who have the energy to spare.

In this chapter my principal object is to give a conspectus of the times of the take, quoting my authorities in case the reader has seen only the literature of the eight-hour-day men. I have already discussed the evening rise and the overnight taking times as these are "special". This leaves us with a considerable period of the day to consider.

The most important take during this period, the one on which the eight-hour angler, whether he knows it or not, principally depends, is the noonday rise. It occurs quite regularly on most days from the beginning to the end of the season, varying in start and duration according to weather and time of year. It can almost be relied on, unlike the celebrated evening rise, which is perhaps more of an obsession with anglers than a dependable experience even of those days on which it occurs. "If I were forced to choose one hour, and only one," says Earl Grey, "in which to fish daily throughout the season, it would be this hour from twelve to one o'clock."

In April, on a good day (say, 12° C), it will be nicely up to time, or even a little early. I vividly remember, however, a fishing holiday on the Annan in the first week of the season when, in spite of sleet and even snow, Large Spring Olives came on the water every day punctually at half-past one, and for a little while the fun was fast and furious. Nothing happened either before or after this delayed noonday rise.

Grey, whose experience was mostly in the south, tells us: "The real rise must not be expected till eleven o'clock or later, and any slackness of sport, at any rate up to twelve o'clock, need not be regarded as prejudicing in the least the prospects of the day." He admits: "I do, however, become anxious if at one o'clock there is still no rise."

A ten o'clock start in April, therefore, will give the angler the opportunity to get his hand in on the occasional risers before the main chance of the day presents itself on either side of noon.

Even in May a considerable rise before ten o'clock is improbable but, when it happens, it can be very worthwhile, as the trout seem to have more abandon than later in the day. Stewart is very reliable for Scottish experience: "We have never at this season found it of any use to attempt fly-fishing before seven or eight in the morning: the forenoon, from eight till about noon or an hour or two after, we consider the best time; about two they generally leave off taking, but commence again in the evening, if the weather is mild." In a good May, therefore, we may have a second take, an early evening rise, some time between six and, at latest, eight o'clock.

By the end of this month, too, the noonday rise tends to spread out or become a series of rises, following each other so closely as to seem almost continuous. But the gap between the extended noon and the early evening rises is usually very distinct. The eight-hour angler, having no hope of an evening rise proper so early in the year, may pack up too soon and miss an important chance. On ideal days, when the temperature may reach 16° in the shade, nine or ten hours would make a more profitable day. It will allow time off for a meal between four and six o'clock.

The doldrums, mid-June to mid-August, are the despair of beginners and holiday anglers to whom the evening rise and the big fly of night prove too difficult or too inconvenient. Both have been treated separately in previous chapters. As for the noon-day rise, it continues to give some diminished opportunities but hardly justifies a full day's fishing, and the early evening rise is usually absent.

Nevertheless, these are not the only possibilities of this time of year, as was well known to our forefathers. In fact, it may be said that angling literature itself began in the sunny days of high summer, early in the morning. I quote the opening lines of *The Arte of Angling* (anonymous, 1577):

"Viator: What, friend Piscator, are you even at it so early?

"Piscator: Yea, the proverb is truly in me verified: early up and never the near; all the speed is in the morning"—by which I think he meant that however early you rise is never early enough.

Many of the later classical authors have advocated the earliest part of the day at this season, but it is notable that few of the moderns are particularly enthusiastic.

The late Oliver Kite usually began "about 9.30, but", he says, "I sometimes catch trout about 8 a m at this time of year (July), and you may even see them busy with Broadwings at sun up"— a useful tip.

G E M Skues is even more helpful: "All the spinners do not die and fall spent on the water over night. Some come on to the water in the cool of the early norning, and if the angler tries in the hot weather for an early morning trout, the spinner may be commended to him as giving him his best chance, so far as floating patterns are concerned. And when, before the rise comes

on, an odd fish or so may be found in position putting up occas-
sionally at something, spinners may legitimately be suspected."

Judicious remarks such as these may not be sufficiently stimulating to get the ordinary angler out of bed in the early hours.
The spur of enthusiasm is needed, and it comes from one of our
up-to-date writers, W. B. Currie: "The early morning rise is a
delight. One is alert in the cool summer air at five or six o'clock
in June or July in a way that seems impossible at any other
time of day. The trout feed with a steadiness which reminds me
of spring fishing, and both dry and wet fly take well fished upstream in the thin water. . . . There is usually a distinct rise in
the morning, beginning around dawn and finishing before breakfast time. Sometimes it is all over by seven. While it lasts it is
among the finest things in a dry fly fisher's season."

Therefore, two programmes might be suggested for the dog-
days of July and August; one, an occasional fishing sortie from
dawn to breakfast, extended on auspicious occasions to noon;
and two, an all-night "ordeal" with the big fly, meeting the dawn
rise before going home. This can be very enjoyable.

We come now to the end of the season. Like most other writers,
I am in danger of dismissing September as something of an after-
thought. It is a problem month, badly documented. No one fails
to mention the falling-off in condition of the trout and that the
flies are not really new—the Late March Brown and the Olives.
Indeed, this month has some of the qualities of May and April.
But it has, too, a character of its own.

There is a reservoir of heat in both earth and water, which
makes a difference, but not much has been recorded about the
effects. There is, therefore, scope for some field study of taking
times in September.

W H Lawrie is of further help to Scottish anglers, at least.
He recommends a second spell of night fishing which becomes
possible around the time of the harvest moon. And that's about
all. Consequently, most anglers, as yet, seem as disinclined from a
twenty-four week season for their sport as they are from a twenty-
four hour day.

This concludes my conspectus of taking times. For ease of
reference it is summarised in the table at the end of this chapter.

All times are, of course, approximate. Those in the body of
the chapter are Greenwich but in the table I have used British

Summer Time, which is one hour ahead. B S T makes it easier to
get at the early morning trout but postpones the later rises.

Trout Taking Times

Weeks	Months	Takes	Times (B S T)
1–6	April/May	Noon rise	11 am to 3 pm
7–10	May/June	Extended noon rise	10 am to 5 pm
		Early evening rise	7 pm to 8 pm
11–18	June/July/August	Dawn-to-breakfast rise	4 am to 10 am
		Noon rise	11 am to 1 pm
		Early evening rise	7 pm to 8 pm
		Evening rise	9 pm to midnight
		Big fly at night	11 pm to dawn
19–24	August/September	Extended noon rise	10 am to 5 pm
		Second night fly at harvest moon	8 pm to —

PART VI

Other Ways

[20]

Grayling

. . . they say he feeds on Gold.   IZAAK WALTON

Since Walton's day the grayling seems to have changed sex. Most writers refer to *her* rather than *him* and I propose to do the same just for the fun of it; for that is my main attitude to the grayling; for me she is a creature of fun, though sometimes the fun runs a bit thin.

I first met her on the Annan, punctually at half-past one every day of the first week of a long ago April when she and the trout together came on the rise to Spring Olives. For half an hour or so I took both fish alternately from the same stream. Her average weight, I noticed, was greater than the trout's, though the really big fish are usually trout. Thus I came to know her considerable charms: her elegant proportions, her firm, sequin-mailed form, her magnificent tartan plaid of a dorsal fin and, behind it, the adipose tag that enrols her in the salmon clan. I never recovered, though her favours since then have been sparing and my fidelity has barely survived her inexhaustible superciliousness. If game fishing is an exasperating pleasure, the grayling is the sport's epitome.

My ticket for certain waters strictly insists that I kill every grayling I catch, irrespective of size or season, a rule I have painful scruples about. I take great care not to catch them in the trout season and in the other part of the year to catch only the bigger fish. When I fail in these objectives, I don't incriminate myself by confessing what I do. I like grayling and am grateful to her for many enjoyable experiences, and I forgive her for the others. I don't grudge her a share of the trout's water. I regret that my expeditions into the Highlands beyond the Tay and its tributaries take me beyond her range. South of the Tay, right down to the English Channel, there are few notable rivers for trout that don't have their complement of grayling. Wherever the water is clear and the substratum gravel or sand the grayling will flourish, some allege, at the expense of the trout; but their habits are sufficiently diverse to make no more necessary than some thinning of their numbers here and there. Happily she is almost impossible to eradicate, except by means of pollution, for which her tolerance is less than the trout's.

She breeds in April or May, which means she is in season during the autumn and winter, providing the trout fisherman with an extension of his sport, for grayling may be regarded as the trout's alternative. They feed in much the same way and on similar items. If twenty-four weeks' fishing are not enough you can add a few more, with interesting variations of method. There are many pleasant days in autumn, and winter is not always the harsh durance it seems when you stay at home and complain.

Grayling differ from trout in another important respect. They tend to shoal, whereas trout, however plentiful they may be in a given area, hold their positions individually. Big grayling seem somewhat more solitary than the smaller ones; but I cannot be sure of this. Though I have caught big ones as single spies, I have also caught them successively from the same pool or stream. Generally speaking, the main problem in grayling fishing is to locate them, which is easy in clear water or when they are surface feeding, but at other times much more difficult. A pool in which you caught a dozen last week when the water was low may give you nothing at all after some days of rain. The shoal has moved, and may be very hard to find again. The fly fisher will have to prospect the stream, looking for the shadows in the depths or for the multitudinous dimples on the surface, so different from the more scattered rises of the trout. Experience will help him to recognise the whereabouts of his quarry. He will not linger in the rocky parts, though the grayling likes fast water when in season: wherever a strong stream merges into a broad flat or pool with a gravelly bottom, that's where she will mostly be found. She lies deeper than the trout and more in open water. It is unusual to find her hugging the bank or occupying the obstructed holes and corners so beloved of the trout. Perhaps she prefers room around her for her companions: perhaps she likes a wider lookout. By lying deep in the stream she achieves the latter object in a different way: her normal window through the surface must be much wider than the trout's. Perhaps she is more long-sighted, which could explain a lot.

The fisherman sometimes gets the impression that she is tormenting him personally by playing catch as catch can. Most writers make excuses for her. They say she is a bad aimer, apt to miss her target, which seems inconsistent with nature's law of economy. True, she comes up in a steep rise from a deeper lie than the trout and has a smaller mouth for her instrument of capture. Perhaps we meet her midway in a stage of her evolution; perhaps she took to surface-fly diet a few million years later than the trout; perhaps she sees her prey better from a distance but gets it out of focus at the moment of seizure. Whatever the explanation, most authorities assert she will rise repeatedly and get stuck only at the umpteenth attempt. Again I can't be so sure. I've caught many grayling at successive first offers on favourable days—that is, when *she* is favourable. On other and more common occasions she proves herself an expert rejectress. She takes advantage of your hand, conditioned in a season of trout fishing. Your reactions are too deliberate. Paused striking is all right for trout, but she needs split-second timing. If our autumn streams were clearer, so that we could observe her ascent from the gravel, things might be easier for us.

The grayling has been given very little attention by scientists. Consequently she is still a legendary fish. There's the one about her soft mouth. What a nonsense! It's a tough rubber washer. It's not that the hook breaks free; it just so often fails to penetrate. Another is about her fragrance of thyme which I haven't the nose to dispute, though a bagful of grayling have a very distinctive, and not unpleasant, fishy smell as anyone might suppose. As thyme is often used at the cooking stage it may be associated with the newly caught fish by a sort of anticipatory metathesis. But the story of her dorsal trigger is a bit much. Listen to this from a well-known contemporary writer: "They dart up almost perpendicularly from the bottom. In this they are aided by a peculiar air bladder which works in conjunction with the back fin. When the latter is erected the bladder fills with air and deflates again when the fin subsides." He omits to explain where the extra air comes from. For me, I just don't believe in the grayling's instantaneously self-inflating buoyancy vest.

Then there's the legend that she's uneatable, which rationalises some of the hatred she seems to inspire in many anglers. Out of season, certainly, she is no great delicacy, but in autumn and winter I, for my part, like her better than trout at their best. Her flesh is always white but firm and curdy. Even in May (dare I say it?) trout are not always as palatable as everyone is in a conspiracy to maintain. In her own season the grayling is always delicious.

Walton's legend that she feeds on gold may derive from our ancestors' estimation of her value as a sporting or edible fish: or else, it may have something to do with her well-known interest in tinselled artificial flies. Which brings me to a consideration of her food and how to fish for her.

She likes quite a variety of protein, even occasionally responding to a spun minnow, which might seem, therefore, a likely means of attaining a record-sized fish. Happily, I don't think that's necessary. Although many fishers, especially in winter, go after her with bait, usually worm or maggot, she provides excellent sport with fly. The largest of trout tend to go off fly diet for reasons that can readily be imagined: but grayling seem less inclined to change their diet as they grow; at any rate, there are quite frequent occasions when big grayling will take the smallest of flies, whereas big trout often lose interest in all but the large sedges or Mayflies, which are special to particular times. Of course grayling never attain the proportions of the largest trout. A two pounder is a good fish, a three pounder exceptional, and four pounds near to a record. I have not caught any bigger than about two and a half pounds, which, for me therefore, is a big fish. I caught that one on dry fly in early spring.

Special flies are often recommended. These usually incorporate gold or silver tinsel and coloured tags. This perhaps is always the primitive stage of any kind of fly fishing when attraction rather than deception is the fisherman's main objective. Certainly, grayling flies can be very successful. But in recent years there has been a growing tendency to present the grayling with careful representations of the insects she feeds on—exactly the same fare as the trout's—and the results justify the practice at least most of the time. Because of her small mouth and her readiness to reject or eject what she dislikes, the smallest possible representations of the natural insects are thought to be advisable, whereas a common principle in trout fishing is to use the largest fly the trout will readily accept. I only have recourse to the more fancy kind of grayling fly nowadays as a final desperation: I find my success assured by the same range of artificial flies as I use for trout, offered in the same ways, under, on, and in the surface. Nymph fishing for grayling is again the predominant method: but dry fly can be practised during a greater proportion of productive time than is the case with trout. Trout may persist at the nymphal stage: grayling almost always show willingness to continue the take above the surface when duns begin to appear. The grayling, therefore, is a good friend to the dry-fly specialist. Even in winter, when a sunny spell encourages a hatch of that most adaptable fly, the Large Spring Olive, an hour or two of dry fly is often possible. In November, when the L S O is at its most numerous, grayling often continue feeding on it well into the evening dusk.

On the rough streams in winter, trotting a small red worm downstream with the help of a small float is a favourite method which I like to use when fly fishing is not practicable. Alternatively, Sawyer's Grayling Bug, which is a sort of nymph tied with a wool body and which is, perhaps, the modern equivalent of the so-called Grasshopper, popular a century ago, may be tried, fished deep. I keep promising myself to try it. Coming from such an expert source I have no doubt it will be a very effective alternative fly-fishing method.

A few minor variations of trout-fishing tactics should be noted. Grayling may seem less easily scared. With reasonable care the fisherman may continue to fish the same pool for a considerable time, catching several grayling without much change of position. In fact, change may be dangerous: once an outlier grayling has been frightened into the security of the main stream, the panic may spread to the whole shoal, putting them off the feed or on the way to safer areas.

It is common experience to catch a few grayling, getting quite frequent offers for some duration of time, and then to find the sport abruptly terminated. Perhaps the shoal has just moved on: but usually, if the pool is rested for half an hour, the take begins again; which suggests rather that the fish had become alerted.

The little man who for some years served as river watcher on one of my favourite waters once demonstrated how a shoal may be panicked. He approached the tail of a very productive pool just as I reached its head. The silly man, who was not employed for his knowledge of fish or fishing, thought to do me a good turn. He came along the edge of the bank towards me, waving his arms and cap over the water. Looking down into the side slack I could see the dark shadows of numerous grayling scurrying in panic up and down until they all vanished into the obscurity of the deep water at the neck of the stream. These startled fish were a small proportion of the total shoal whose outliers were being scared into flight by the idiotic antics of that stupid man. He explained that he was sending the fish up to me! I didn't thank him: I threatened to report his behaviour to the association secretary, which, of course, I didn't. The next time I met him he gave me some very confident advice on choice of fly, which, no doubt, he had picked up from other anglers, but which I appreciated about as much as you may suppose.

Because of their tendency to lie low in the water, not poising as trout do just under the surface, it is advisable to present the fly well above the position where a rise may be expected. This allows the fly to appear at the edge of the grayling's window and to give her time to come up to meet it as it floats down. Several yards above is not too much. Indeed, drifting the dry fly downstream, paying out line or moving down at the speed of the current to keep the fly afloat, is a tactic that can be practised on grayling more often and more successfully than on trout. Similarly, when nymphing or fishing wet fly, it often pays to extend the time of a cast by letting the fly drift downstream past the angler and into lower water already fished. I have often caught grayling by this tactic when the upstream cast alone has failed, presumably because the fish had not seen the fly when it alighted too close to its position, but did so later on when I had moved upwards and gave it another chance by letting the fly drift down to it. These special considerations in regard to fly presentation for grayling argue also for longer casting than is usual for trout. At least I have formed the habit of keeping farther away from the grayling and it seems to pay off. The fact that they tend to station themselves well away from the bank means longer casting by anyone who is not wading.

The trout fisher, new to grayling fishing, will find playing the fish a rather different experience. She has been very unfairly aspersed by those who resent her presence. Even Charles Cotton

who loved her (after a fashion), libelled her inexcusably, calling
her "the deadest hearted of fishes". That's a midsummer fallacy.
Get a good grayling on a fine line in autumn or winter and you'll
have power to deal with—hydraulic power; for she doesn't take
to the air (except, they say, in the Arctic). She turbines into the
heavy stream for which she is better equipped than the trout. Or
she erects her back fin, like a sail, and tacks across the current at
right angles. If you have ever tried to turn a boat caught like this
in the tide, you will appreciate the force she can exert against your
efforts to bring her head round. Because she fights so whole-
heartedly, never, like the trout, seeking refuge among rocks or
weeds, never sulking like the salmon, she quickly exhausts her
strength. Nevertheless, because she more often succeeds in getting
or keeping below the angler, the attempt to draw her over the net
should be made very cautiously; a last-minute drive across stream
is only too likely; and a sudden tightening of a fine line with a
tiny hook-hold by a fish whose weight she knows how to maxi-
mise by spreading her dorsal against the current of the river,
frequently gives her freedom at the end of the struggle. "Oh me,
look you Master, a fish a fish! Oh las, Master, I have lost her!"
In your paradox of fishing pleasure the grayling will give you all
the anxiety and heartbreak you could wish for.

I almost love the grayling, as I have tried to show. The hatred
she inspires in many others, rationalise it how they will, is beyond
reason: but once I was thankful for it. On a lovely September day
I found myself, on Clyde, fishing slowly downstream from pool
to flat behind a brother of the angle whose skill seemed much
greater than mine. For every fish I caught he caught three or
four, trout and grayling. I kept both species; but he, with spectacular bad temper, tossed every grayling on to the bank, whence
I quickly retrieved it. That day I was young enough to rejoice in a
bulging bagful of the grey beauties such as I have never since
equalled. But, of course, I prefer to catch my own; and when
autumn comes and the trout begin to pall on me, even sometimes
before the legal end of the season, I begin to think again about
grayling, planning a new campaign, though I am nagged with all
too familiar apprehensions of another exasperating game of
catch as catch can.

L

Still Water Revolution

As far as still water is concerned we are standing on the threshold of imitative fly fishing. GEOFFREY BUCKNALL

A sort of transvaluation of all values has taken place in attitudes to trout fishing. Old prejudices and snobberies which usurped the name of art have, partly in the name of science, given way to new tolerances. Dry-fly fishing long ago left the chalk stream preserves and wet fly returned there from the despised rough streams of the north and west. Still water fishing, the humblest branch of trout fishing, is today coming into its own. Whether it is the last in a series of reappraisals, or just the latest example, I don't know; but this is certain: any writer who relegates the subject to the last chapter or two of a book on trout fishing is under obligation to apologise and explain.

Still water fly fishing is no longer a minority sport: more people are now fishing the lakes, reservoirs and gravel pits of populous England than the diminishing streams: and in Scotland, though river fishing is still the majority sport, there are more square miles of loch than of river, and in the holidays these are invaded by thousands of eager and ever more knowledgeable fishers. Still water fishing cannot be dismissed as an extra with the implication of being of less value. Fortunately, today there is a surge of interest in this branch, and talented fishermen, many of them with scientific qualifications, are rapidly raising it from the primitive to the sophisticated level on which it can claim equality with its predecessors. This is why I can expect forgiveness for devoting only two chapters to the subject: they are intended, not as dismissal of a minor matter, but as introduction to a study and practice which deserve much more prolonged attention. If, like me, the reader begins on the river, or spends more of his time there, he will find two chapters on still water fly fishing useful as introduction to yet another branch of the sport, as long as it is still a secondary interest: as soon as he begins, by choice or necessity, to pursue still water fly fishing as a main hobby, then a mere inroduction will cease to be adequate: he must, in that case, have recourse to the excellent full-length treatments which are now appearing. I list some of these in the appendix.

I am inclined to the view expressed by C F Walker in *Lake Flies and their Imitation* that still water fly fishing began as a diminished form of sea-trout fishing: the traditional methods and the flies used were not designed for the brown trout: and this second-hand tradition is a very recent one, going no farther back than the last century. Still water fishing seems to have no tradition of its own and river fly fishing has undergone several transformations in quite recent times; but, as I have been at pains to maintain, it has a long rich tradition of its own and its modern developments have been, for the most part, drawn from it rather than added to it. The contemporary experiments on still water are very different. The new things are being introduced to it from outside, mainly from the riverside tradition, partly from practices evolved abroad, and even from traditions very alien to trout fishing at all. Many new recruit to trout fishing are men who have fished for lifetimes in canals and broads for roach, bream, carp and other coarse fish. They have come to trout fishing without any trout sophistication. They have applied fresh minds to new problems and some of their solutions are proving quite revolutionary. Still water trout fishing is at a very exciting stage of change which may take a generation or more to become stabilised. Several contending factions may be identified as follows:

1. "Traditional" wet-fly fishing.
2. Modern representational fly fishing.
3. Dry-fly fishing.
4. Large lure fishing.

Wet-fly Fishing

The fishing-tackle shop will offer a thousand beautiful confections in exchange for money; and some of these devices which go by the name of flies have acquired reputations. No doubt they all catch trout. Whether the popular ones catch more trout because they are fished more or are fished more because they are more successful is an impossible question. A novice loch fisher may quite confidently accept the shopkeeper's recommendation or, perhaps better, more local opinion. He will almost certainly be persuaded to use Butcher, Teal and Red, Teal and Green, Peter Ross, Alexandra, Grouse and Claret, Red Palmer, Soldier Palmer, Zulu, Dunkeld—to name only a few. They will all sometime, somewhere catch fish, if used in suitable ways. Such flies may at one time have had representational bases, echoing the colours and forms of underwater life—nymph, beetle, small fish. If so, their secret origins have been lost. Undoubtedly they often deceive fish, though the deception may be accidental. Equally often their success is to be attributed to the stimulus they give to the trout's rapacity. A hungry trout will seek its food by patient hunting. Occasionally it will respond to a sudden stimulus which suggests food—movement, sparkle. It may have no leisure to repent an access of curiosity or rage. Standard loch flies, therefore, tend to catch the occasional fish who happens to be in an experimental, or irritable, mood. Representational flies, on the other hand, are designed to deceive the trout in its normal food-seeking activities and are likely to be more generally success-ful. On the remoter lochs, where wild trout still predominate and where food organisms are perhaps less plentiful or various, standard patterns of non-representational flies such as those given above may prove very successful, which is no doubt the main reason for the persistence of standard or traditional practices in those waters.

In still water, even where wind and tributary streams provide some movement, trout have to rove as they forage for food. The space they inhabit is enormous. It is much more difficult to determine by surface observation where trout are to be found. Local knowledge, one's own or a boatman's, is very useful. These are reasons why boat fishing is very popular on still water. A knowledgeable boatman is the best assurance of sport on a strange loch.

The main technique is to cast a team of flies down wind as the boat drifts over the favoured area and to retrieve the flies by a fairly rapid raising of the rod towards the vertical. Many loch fishers seem quite content with this repetitive procedure.

Some vary it by changing the angle of cast, or by breaking the continuity of the retrieve into a number of consecutive sink-and-draw movements: but the drift of the boat may be too fast for this desirable method of fishing to be possible. The objective is to fish the tail-fly under the water, the middle-fly somewhere near the surface, and the top-bob tripping the crests of the ripples. Thus the trout are offered three various inducements. Two things are considered essential: there must be a ripple; and the flies must be kept on the move; otherwise there is unlikely to be any response from the fish. A very enjoyable day may be spent thus. Some or many trout may be caught. The family may enjoy the outing as much as the fisherman himself.

But the whole procedure is often wearisome in the extreme. Bad weather, which fishermen learn to accept, can be much more uncomfortable or even dangerous, experienced in an open boat. What is even more difficult to thole is the frequent failure of the whole method. It is so much a matter of repetitive casting of trial and error offerings that only success can make it tolerable as fishing. It satisfies little of the other characteristics of the serious angler: it offers nothing to his understanding and the only intellectual gain is from the talk that may accompany it. No wonder so many writers on loch fishing like to tell stories about Sean and Duncan, who gillied for them so philosophically in Connemara or Sutherland.

Standard wet-fly fishing may be practised also from the bank or by wading. This makes it much more respectable from the intellectual point of view. The angler is more likely to be on his own. He will be reading the indications of the shore line and the depths and shallows into which he is casting his flies. He will not be casting so much at random and will often be covering the rises of individual fish; or by reading the direction of its travel from the surface indications will be practising the still water art of presenting his flies in the path of a roving trout. Since most feeding trout are likely to be in the shallower waters near the shore, the wading fisherman is more often in position to exploit these feeding areas. Experiments of all kinds are easier for him. He can vary the speed of his retrieves and discover the most successful. He can even begin to observe closely what the trout are taking and so prepare his mind for other methods of fishing which take the trout's food into account.

Representational Fly

I am rather proud to be able to record that the first article I ever wrote on fishing, which was printed in the *Edinburgh Evening News* early in the 1920s, was an original advocacy of small flies for the loch. That I had natural representations in mind is shown by the fact that I used a cross heading "Catering to Taste", which the editor altered to "Getting the right fly". I was recommending that loch fishers should abandon big flashy flies and use river patterns, such as Greenwell and Hare's Ear, instead. I had proved their effectiveness. Two small streams, on which I had learned my fly fishing, had their origins in two reservoirs within walking distance of home. I liked to fish right up at the overflow from the dams: for in the first pools of the streams one could expect in early spring to find large trout which had escaped or been swept out of the lochs. Sometimes I climbed the dams and had a go in the forbidden waters above, discovering by this chance that still water fish were quite enthusiastic about my small wingless spiders. Later on, when I could afford the necessary permits, I continued my experiments and was seldom less successful than my companions who were usually prejudiced in favour of bigger and flashier lures. I reacted strongly in favour of my small flies and earned twopence a line by writing about them.

Of course, I was only indirectly fishing with representations; for I knew nothing about the insects of the still waters. Greenwell's Glory is not known to be representational, though it may have been designed after the Large Spring Olive, or Olive Dun of our forefathers, which does not occur in still water. Fortunately for me in the 'twenties, and for others today, it and many other river representations have proved very effective on still water by the happy chance that some of the natural day flies of still water closely resemble their cousins of the running streams. Thus, artificial nymphs, duns, and spinners, dressed to imitate river insects, may serve another turn. On those days when trout are taking day flies at any stage of development the river fisher need have no depair about "catering to taste".

Which does not mean that loch fishing is merely a matter of transferring river practices to the still water. Some of the day flies are very similar: but day flies are not so numerous on still water and provide a much smaller part of the trout's larder. Other insects and small forms of life fill the rest of it. The contemporary movement, which, as Geoffrey Bucknall says, is still not over the threshold of imitative fly fishing, is discovering and experimenting with a much wider variety of natural food forms. Besides those insects which are traditionally imitated for river fishing—day flies, Mayflies, sedges—and which occur or have counterparts on still water, there are others either unknown on the river or of comparatively little value there for the fisherman. Of these, the broadwings, midges or buzzers, water-boatmen, dragonflies, beetles, and shrimps are the most important. Other insects that have no aquatic connection except as they are much more frequently borne on to still water by the wind, are from time to time significant—ants, daddy-long-legs, terrestrial beetles, dung flies, heather moths—are often of much greater interest to the still water than to the river specialist, though the ordinary or occasional angler will have enough to do learning to use the commoner aquatic inhabitants. Many very beautiful and ingenious representations of these creatures are becoming available from specialist fly tyers: though the angler who has the interest and skill to tie his own is better able to equip himself with a suitable stock of varieties. Press articles and books now appearing give the new recipes and the modes of fishing them, thus beginning a new stage of fly-fishing tradition that bids fair to enhance the pleasures of our seemingly inexhaustible sport. Representational fly fishing on still water is at an early stage of development, but will quickly mature and attain parity with its river fishing counterpart.

In my opinion it will take precedence over all other methods, without necessarily ousting its rivals, because it appeals to a richer variety of intellectual interests than the others.

In the next chapter I shall be more specific about the flies of the still water which are being successfully imitated and about the methods used: but before I leave the subject of representational fly fishing, a few words about T C Ivens's contribution to contemporary experiment would be appropriate at this point. Actually he makes a bold compromise between standard and representational practices. He asserts the primacy of wet fly for the still waters, maintaining that floating insects form a minimal part of the diet of the trout. He distinguishes between "attractor" flies and "deceivers", both of which are to be used according to circumstances, as soon as fish are found on the feed the deceivers being the likelier choice. Ivens is a logical thinker who has worked out his ideas in every detail. He recommends very slow recovery of deceiver flies, since natural insects do not move fast, and distant casting for which he believes in a long rod to supply the power. He has designed both rod and flies for his method of fishing which may be considered specially applicable for the new large reservoirs that are a feature of today's water supply systems.

His deceiver flies are not strictly representational: they are like the Greenwell in this respect, being general, rather than specific, in their resemblance to natural insects. I think Ivens has little respect for the cult of close imitation, being more interested in classes of insects with similar characteristics than in particular ones. Yet he is not a careless observer and his specimens are very carefully designed. When I first tried them, soon after his book was published, what chiefly worried me was the large hook sizes he recommended. These I conservatively, perhaps wrongly, reduced in the summer months for fishing my own reservoirs where I had little hope of extra big fish: but I found the larger ones quite effective there in spring and very much so in the lochs of Orkney where I had a holiday in the summer. As I write, Ivens is publishing a second edition of his book which may renew interest, mine and others', in his special contribution to still water fly-fishing development. Meantime, I confess that, having absorbed some of it into my practice, I am more attracted to the school of representation associated with such names as C F Walker, Frank Goddard, Geoffrey Bucknall, and John Henderson.

Dry Fly

There are those who deny the effectiveness of dry-fly fishing on still waters and others who believe in it passionately. Much depends on the places being fished. On some waters it is a rare occurrence to see a general rise to surface fly; whereas a visitor from the chalk streams would be very happy on some others, though he would have, perhaps, to learn the new trick of fishing the path, rather than the rise, of a feeding fish.

It might be thought that dry flies for the still water would necessarily be representational, as they are on the river, copies in fur and feather of actual duns and spinners. This has not always been the case. Many dry flies used on the lochs bear no resemblance to specific insects: it has been claimed that anything bushy enough to float for long periods, during which it survives an occasional tweak or drag to simulate life, is good enough. If we include dapping under the heading of dry fly, this indifference to representation reaches the extreme. Loch Ordie and other daps resemble nothing I know in nature and depend for success on their size and buoyancy. All these primitive dry flies can be successful; but the reader will not be surprised when I tell him that modern development is away from the primitive and towards closer representation in size, form, and colour, of the insects likely to be found floating on the surface. This brings still water dry-fly fishing out of its isolation and makes it part of representational fly fishing which, as on the river, is practised under, on, and in the surface, as will be shown in the next chapter. Nevertheless, the use of dapping with Loch Ordies or Daddy-long-legs creations is often very successful, especially on Highland and Irish lochs, and should sometimes be tried on the artificial waters nearer home.

Large Lure Fishing

Although I have always been ready to have a go at any interesting form of fishing, and believe in the open mind, this is one development which has not yet excited me. Perhaps if I had to fish on the large new artificial dams of the south, stocked with rainbows as well as brown trout, and fished by converts from the coarse-fishing tradition, I would be happy to conform. From the security of distance and success with other methods, I am inclined, like Geoffrey Bucknall, to regard large lure fishing as a desperate violation of the no-spinning rule and outwith the spirit of fly fishing. Nevertheless, I acknowledge the resource and ingenuity of the new men who have discovered and exploited this new branch of the sport.

Again, it seems to have come down from another tradition, namely from sea-trout practice in estuarial waters, with some other contributions from America.

In the short period of ten years, large lure fishing has established itself on the extensive new reservoirs of England. Already two distinct methods have emerged, which may be distinguished as

the fast-surface and the slow-deep methods. These have neces-
sitated lines which float, or sink quickly and deep, to suit each
style: and a special technique of extra long casting, using a
synthetic or silk shooting head of about 30 feet attached to nylon
monofilament backing. Both methods are practised from the shore
by wading anglers. Very long casts are usually necessary, perhaps
because of the large numbers of anglers who scare the fish away
from the shores, but more because of the need to conserve energy
by reducing the number of casts and to cover as many trout as
possible.

Fast stripping or recovery is the essential feature of the first
method: and to collect the spare line as it is gathered down from
the rod rings the fishermen have a floating raft tethered to their
left side on which the line is coiled. This prevents it becoming
waterlogged and assists the next long cast. Many fishermen seem
to assume that the lures cannot be too quickly stript in and the
job becomes quite furious: but others experiment with different
speeds of retrieve.

By the slow-deep method the lures are allowed to sink, sometimes to the very bottom, which may require a pause of several
minutes after each cast. Thereafter the lures are brought back by
slow or very, very slow, pulls on the line. Because of the obvious
danger, by this method, of hooking the bottom, special weedless
lures have been invented. These have fine wire or nylon filaments
that ward the hooks off underwater obstructions.

The lures themselves are now very various. They may be single,
tandem, or three-hook creations, utilising feather, hair, or synthetic materials. Many of them are a return to sea-trout or even
salmon fly patterns and sizes: others may have smaller counterparts among the standard loch flies of the past, or be wholly new
creations. Their names sometimes give clues to their origins:
Conon Lure, Dunkeld, Three Rivers, Fraser, Muddler Minnow.

A special series of large lures which have been deliberately
designed to represent small fish fry may bring part of this method
under the heading of representational fly fishing; for the term
"fly" has always been a very unspecific one. These are the
"polystickles", whose chief exponent is Dick Walker. They began
as imitations of sticklebacks, but there are now available minnow,
roach, perch, and many other stickles. Because the success of
several traditional loch flies was almost certainly due to their

resemblance to small fry, a series of "traditional" polystickles has been designed after the patterns of such old favourites as the Peter Ross, and Alexandra. Further experiments of this kind are certain to follow as long as new waters are being opened up for fishing, or if fertilisation by modern methods is successful in maintaining stocks of very large fish. Wherever brown trout share their habitat with coarse fish, the larger they grow the more likely they are to become fry-feeders during some part of the year at least; and rainbow trout, which are favourite stock fish, seem naturally more interested in large food and less inclined to hunt the surface levels for the smaller organisms usually imitated by fly fishers. During the early years of new waters, when fish grow rapidly to exceptional sizes, large lure fishing is certain to be fashionable. If, as used to happen with management methods of the past, the production of large fish tapers off in later years, the use of big and multiple hook lures may also decline. Time will tell.

[22]

Flies for the Still Water

There are so many sorts of Flies . . . and their breeding is so various and wonderful, that I might easily amaze myself and tire you in the relation of them.   IZAAK WALTON

My purpose in this chapter is to do for the still water what I did for the river in Chapter 16; that is, to provide a list of flies and suitable representations and some advice on how to fish them such as would enable an inexperienced fisherman to approach the waterside with a degree of confidence at any part of the season. It is at once an easier and a more difficult purpose to perform satisfactorily. For one thing the sheer amount of insect life on which the trout subsist in still water is vastly greater than in the river and the variety corresponds. On the other hand, much of this life is too minute for imitation on hooks large enough for fishing and the habits of the tiny creatures are usually just as impossible to simulate by rod and line management. This effectively reduces the practical range of selection. Furthermore, much less study and experiment has been done on the insect life of the still waters and one can recommend only what very contemporary experts have so far described and tried out. Even so, during recent years the list has been growing steadily and the methods of the century-old flasher-fly tradition are being vigorously challenged.

There is no reason why a beginner to still water fishing should not arm himself with traditional flies. Grouse and Claret, Peter Ross, Butcher, Alexandra will catch him many a trout. Somewhat more modern attractors of the Ivens type, such as the Jersey Herd, Green and Brown Nymph, and Black and Peacock Spider, may be added to the contents of the fly box. After some practice at slow sink-and-draw fishing with these he should extend his interest to the representational type of fly and immediately, I believe, he will feel he is getting on terms of intimacy with the trout. Only then will he begin to relish the essential immorality of fly fishing and, like Charles Cotton, achieve the angler's "ambition to be one of the greatest deceivers".

Essential reading for this approach are Jocelyn Lane's *Lake and Loch Fishing for Trout,* C F Walker's *Lake Flies and their Imitation,* and Goddard's *Trout Flies of Still Water.* There are several other notable contributors—Richard Walker, Geoffrey Bucknall and the head of the firm which supplies fly-tying materials, John Veniard, who are all presently working in this important field of practical research. The next few years, for anyone taking up loch fishing and willing to learn as well as fish, should be as intellectually stimulating as any other period in angling history. I could wish I was a young man again.

Day flies, the ephemeroptera, are much less numerous on still water than on the river and perhaps for that reason less important to the fisherman: but they are the easiest to represent artificially and to fish successfully. Here are some notes on fishing methods which apply generally to the day flies.

Methods of Fishing Day Flies

The same principles as for river fishing apply for the still water. Nymphs are fished mostly in the upper layers with the help of a floating line. It is always necessary when fishing nymph or wet fly to give some movement to the flies. The fisherman should experiment. Generally the retrieve should be quite slow after an initial pause to let the flies sink to the desired depth. Drawing the line in little pulls by means of the left hand is usually better than only raising the rod, as it helps to keep the flies travelling at the desired depth below the surface. Speeds of retrieve should be varied. One writer recommends that recovery might some-times be as slow as half an hour per cast! The varying habits of the natural nymphs, about which information is available in the more detailed literature, is the best guide to such tactics, for some are active and some very laboured swimmers. When several flies are mounted (which may be useful for preliminary exploration) no one speed or method of recovery is likely to suit them all. As soon as possible, therefore, the fisherman should rationalise his leader and specialise with one fly or one type of fly. From the information given above and from the conspectus given later it should be noted that some patterns can do multiple service. In a few years this kind of fishing may become much more puristic, with specific imitations of insects and their stages: even now it is possible, though perhaps not necessary, to specialise, thanks to the accurate inventions of C F Walker and others who have followed his lead.

Dry-fly fishing on the lake is a much less active job than on the river and may therefore make a less popular appeal. A very singleminded approach is necessary if knowledge and skill are to be acquired. The dry fly may seem uncalled for. Its occasions are fewer and the trout are often ready to double on nymph and dun at the same time. It differs from river practice in several ways. As already mentioned, fishing the rise is not usually as successful as on the river: it has to be done rapidly before the cruising fish has moved on. Fishing the path of a cruising trout is not an easier job: it requires a period of observation and may be frustrated in several ways; first, by the "oncer", the fish that rises to the floating fly only very occasionally; second, by the fish that refuses to cruise conveniently along the shore but veers outwards and beyond reach of casting; and third, by the difficulty of knowing, or guessing, the right fly. If the trout are taking midges, it may be useless offering them a dun: but happily this error is not always fatal to success, for surface-feeding fish sometimes prove quite unchoosy. More often, the fisherman does not hunt his fish with the dry fly: he lays it on the surface where he thinks fish are on the move and waits, a long time perhaps, for one to discover it. An occasional tweak of the line helps to attract attention, but otherwise the only movement of the fly is caused by ripples or waves on the surface. In weedy parts, where trout are putting up in small areas of clear water, the dry fly may prove less hazardous than a sinking one and give the fisherman satisfaction from the skill of accurate casting.

In all forms of still-water fly fishing the strike seems to be necessarily slower than on the river. The fish are more deliberate in the take since there is no current to carry away their prey if it is missed. When the strike fails the error is usually in the angler's too quick reaction. Playing a hooked fish is a simpler matter since there is more room. The two most serious problems are: when the fish goes off in a wild unconquerable rush away from the angler so that a long line is drowned and the hook hold thereby weakened: and when the opposite happens, and it runs towards the angler, who has to pull in line very quickly to maintain contact, the reel being too slow for this emergency. If a trout succeeds in getting under the boat it is usually lost and any dropper flies are apt to hook themselves to the keel or thereabouts. Perhaps these typical misfortunes constitute a good case for an automatic, self-wind reel for fishing on still water.

LIST OF DAY FLIES OF STILL WATER

Pond Olive (*Cloëon dipterum*)

DESCRIPTION: Medium large. Very like Medium Olive but darker in colour. Common everywhere.

SEASON: Late May to September.

HOOK SIZE: 12–14.

NYMPH AND WET FLY: Cloëon Nymph (C F Walker), dark Greenwell, Mallard and Claret, P V C Nymph (Goddard).

HATCHING NYMPH: G R H E, Hatching Nymph (Goddard).

DUN: Olive Quill, Greenwell.

SPINNER: Apricot Spinner (Kite), Pond Olive Spinner (Goddard), Sherry Spinner, Lunn's Particular.

NOTES: Nymphs: agile darters: weeds and shallow margins. Spinners best fished in-surface.

Lake Olive (*Cloëon simile*)

DESCRIPTION: Large and dark. Often confused with Pond Olive. Less common.

SEASON: May, June, late August–September.

HOOK SIZE: 13–15.

NYMPH: P V C Nymph (Goddard), fished deep.

DUN AND SPINNER: (Harris) (C F Walker), Greenwell. The dun may be fished wet, near weed beds.

NOTE: Agile darter: weed beds and deeper water.

Sepia Dun (*Leptophlebia marginata*)

DESCRIPTION: Medium large. Dark brown, sepia.

SEASON: April to May. Prefers shallow margins.

HOOK SIZE: 12–13.

NYMPH AND WET FLY: Leptophlebia Nymph (C F Walker), Greenwell, Mallard and Claret.

DUN: Sepia Dun (C F Walker and Kite).

SPINNER: Pheasant Tail, Lunn's Particular.

NOTE: Very useful at beginning of season: probably the cause of my own boyhood success with Greenwell. Laboured swimmer.

Claret Dun (*Leptophlebia vespertina*)

DESCRIPTION: Very similar to Sepia. Walker says he never detected any claret in its colouring nor any significance in its specific name, *vespertina*.

SEASON: May, June and perhaps into July. Continues where Sepia finishes.

HOOK SIZE: 13–14.

NYMPH AND WET FLY: As for Sepia. Pheasant Tail fished deep *or* in-surface.

DUN: Claret Dun (Harris, C F Walker, Henderson), Red Quill.

SPINNER: Claret Spinner (Harris, Henderson), Lunn's Particular.

NOTE: Nymph, laboured swimmer.

Caënis or Broadwing (*Caënis spp*)

This is the Angler's Curse which the river fisher may prefer to ignore as an impossible challenge when it obsesses the trout. It is much more worthy of the lake fisher's attention. Goddard's Last Hope and Skues's Little Marryatt have been recommended for the river and will be useful for unprepared occasions on the loch: but Jocelyn Lane has distinguished two species for more exact representation, namely:

Dusky Broadwing (*C. robusta*)

DESCRIPTION: Tiny white body with darker markings on back. Broad, white wings and three tails.

SEASON: May–August.

HOOK SIZE: 16.

NYMPH: Caënis Nymph (C F Walker or Lane), Footballer (Lane or Bucknall), G R H E. Fish in-surface with very small representations.

DUN AND SPINNER: Caënis Spinner (Lane and Henderson), P W Spinner, Last Hope (Goddard).

Yellow Broadwing (*C. horaria*)

DESCRIPTION: Even smaller than Dusky, body more yellow.
SEASON: June–August.
HOOK SIZE: 17.
NYMPH: As for Dusky.
DUN AND SPINNER: As for Dusky, plus Lunn's Yellow Boy.

Broadwing duns last so short a time that only nymphs and spinners are of any account for fishing, and the nymphs are the more hopeful proposition, taken usually in act of hatching. Whenever duns and spinners are about (transposing on your clothes, hair, or eyelashes!) you can use a nymph with some hope, as the take doesn't seem to be particular as to the stage of development. But there may be so many millions of flies available at the same time; don't expect special favoured customer treatment for your offering. Some anglers just curse and put on a sedge or something else quite different. Movements imparted to nymphs cannot be too minimal. They are silt crawlers in early stages.

OTHER INSECTS

I have necessarily limited the above list of day flies: to it could have been added Blue Winged Olives (see Chapter 16), Autumn Duns and, for Irish loughs and some Scottish lochs, the May Flies. For information about insects of other kinds which may on some waters have particular value for fishing, I think it suitable to refer the reader to more specialist literature; I am thinking especially of such things as Dragon and Damsel Flies, shrimps, water-boatmen, as well as the land-based insects that sometimes arouse the trout's interest: daddy-long-legs, ants, etc. This leaves two important orders, the sedge flies and the midges which even an elementary book may not dismiss. The sedges are old friends and are much the same on still as on running water (the Grannom being the most conspicuous absentee from the latter): so that what was said in Chapter 16 applies very well here. The midges, however, are very special.

Midges (Chironomids)

These are not the biting sort that will undoubtedly plague the fisherman in the last quarter of the season if he ventures to the waterside when the sun is obscured. The chironomids are harm-

M

less, long-legged, hump-backed, gnat-like flies which are becoming recognised today as probably the most important of all insects in the still water trout's larder; and the fisherman who tries to use representations of them will be bang up to date. Jocelyn Lane and C F Walker pioneered this development. Most previous authorities seemed either not to recognise their importance or to despair, like Halford, of imitations that ingeniously copied everything but the essential wriggle. Contemporary writers are less discouraged by the difficulties. The very latest admirable experiments in fly tying and fishing practice are described and illustrated in John Goddard's recent book which is destined to become a classic. I am heavily indebted to him for what follows.

He describes ten varieties of midge which vary in size from large to small and are characterised by colour of adult fly or larva. Although the Blae and Black has probably been taken often for an adult midge and some Blagdon tyings have been popular for many years, adult representations are of only occasional or specialist interest to the fisherman: therefore I think it reasonably restrictive to deal only with the use of early stages, of which the pupa or hatching larva is more valuable than the more immature stages. Thus nymphal representations, mainly red, green, black, or orange, on a hook range from 8 to 12, will possibly cater adequately for most occasions throughout the season. Unfortunately, these tyings are not yet available at the shops. The fisherman must get a specialist to tie them according to recipe or else learn to do it himself: and this emergency might well be the necessary stimulus.

Orange Silver Midge

SEASON: April–May.
HOOK SIZE: 10–12.

Black Midge

SEASON: Early April, July–August.
HOOK SIZE: 12–14.
ADULT: Blae and Black.

Large Red Midge

SEASON: June–August.
HOOK SIZE: 10–12.

Golden Dun Midge

SEASON: Late May–August.
HOOK SIZE: 10–12.

Ribbed Midge

SEASON: May–June, late August, September.
HOOK SIZE: 12.

Blagdon Green Midge

SEASON: All season. Best known: "Blagdon Buzzer".
HOOK SIZE: 14.

Small Brown Midge

SEASON: June–August.
HOOK SIZE: 14–16.

Small Red Midge

SEASON: July–September.
HOOK SIZE: 14–16.

Small Black Midge

SEASON: Early April, June–September.
HOOK SIZE: 16–18.

Fishing with Representations of Midge Larvae

The immature larvae live on or in the bottom. Most of them emerge and become active from time to time and so become available as food for foraging trout. They are small worm-like creatures (blood worms) which move by tail lashing, very difficult to imitate. A single nymphal representation, allowed to sink to the bottom and agitated by tiny rod or line movements, may be successful, especially if the tail parts are made, as Goddard recommends, with carefully chosen, soft curly feather material which may simulate the tail action of the natural insect.

But the best opportunities are when the emergent insects are hanging in the surface film. Pupal representations may be given minimal movements as they lie in-surface. Goddard says only the gentle rocking of the boat is necessary to give sufficient movement to a fly at the end of a short line: but very slow retrieve may also succeed. Goddard's most interesting suggestion is his recommendation of the dropperless leader, greased to float, with several pupal representations strung along and abutting against the blood knots, with this added variation—the hooks should be straight-eyed to allow the flies to hang vertically from the surface tension in the manner of the naturals. The end fly may be a sunk nymph or a dry sedge: the latter would be a good tell tale in dim light and may pay for its own service. I find these suggestions very convincing, though I have still to try them out myself.

The larger midges tend to fly at the extremes of the day: many of the medium and smaller ones in the middle or early evening. When the adult flies are observed in the air or drifting wakelessly and magically over the surface at the bidding of the gentlest breeze, then the fisherman may be fairly confident in fishing with pupal representations in the surface film. The trout are likely to be head-and-tailing conspicuously as they feed on them. There will be millions of real insects, so the odds are formidably against your copy being taken: but perseverance, especially perhaps in limited areas near undisturbed margins, may bring success in warm, calm conditions when sedge flies might be the only alternative.

I am very conscious of the inadequacy of this introduction to a branch of fly fishing which today is of more importance to more fisherman than any other. But beginnings are necessarily brief and incomplete. My best advice is to remember that fly fishing is a great sport, not because it is impossibly difficult, which it isn't, but because it is so rich in its rewards. The true fisherman, at all times, finds intellectual satisfactions no less rewarding than the pleasures of the successful catching of fish. Still water fly fishing today is of special value for both these reasons.

Conspectus of Still Water Flies

Natural Flies	Artificials		
	Spring	Summer	Autumn
Day Flies		*Mayflies*	
	Pond Olive *Lake Olive* Cloëon Nymph (Walker)	*Pond Olive* *Lake Olive* as spring	*Pond Olive* *Lake Olive* as spring

Conspectus of Still Water Flies

Natural Flies	Artificials		
	Spring	Summer	Autumn
Day Flies—*cont.*	dark Greenwell Mallard and Claret PVC Nymph (Goddard) G R H E Hatching Nymph Olive Quill	as spring	as spring
	Sepia Dun *Claret Dun* Leptophlebia Nymph (Walker) Greenwell Mallard and Claret Sepia Dun (Walker and Kite) Pheasant Tail Lunn's Particular Claret Spinner	*Claret Dun* as spring	
Caënis		*Dusky Broad- wing* *Yellow Broad- wing* Caënis Nymph (Walker or Lane) Footballer (Lane) G R H E Caënis Spinner (Lane)	

Conspectus of Still Water Flies

Natural Flies	Artificials		
	Spring	Summer	Autumn
Caënis—*cont.*		P W Spinner Last Hope (Goddard) Lunn's Yellow Boy	
Midges (Chironomids)	*Orange Silver Midge*	*Large Green Midge Large Red Midge Golden Dun Midge*	
	Ribbed Midge		*Ribbed Midge*
	Black Midge |	*Black Midge*	
	Blagdon Green Midge	all season	
		Small Brown Midge |	
		Small Red Midge	
	Small Black Midge	*Small Black Midge*	*Small Black Midge*
Sedge Flies	Various: most of season, see Chapter 16		
Other Flies	*Beetles* *Shrimps*	*Beetles Damsel Flies* *Shrimps Water Boatmen Sticklebacks and other fry*	*Shrimps*
Land Flies		*Ants*	*Daddy-Long- Legs*

PART VII
Experience

Bad Weather in Spring

The flee answers best in the spring.   THOMAS TOD STODDART

So much for the methods and materials of modern fly fishing. I have refrained deliberately from anecdote, which is rather out of date in angling literature today, though I often wonder why. Fishing stories at worst are as good as anything else in a bad book: at their best they illuminate the work of the best writers. Who would wish away from the pages of Grey or Skues those schoolday reminiscences or those authentic tales, very parables of angling, by which the masters charmed us with instruction. Is not this how the literature began? Subtle old Izaak Walton took his reader with him to the waterside, where they talked and fished together in every page of his book. The Angler is Compleat, not as the result of reading, but by the *experience* of angling.

Therefore, I make just a whisper of apology for concluding this book with a few chapters in which instruction takes second place to experience.

When March goes out like a lion and the first days of the trout season are blinded with wind-blown rain or sleet, do you sit patiently at home waiting for a favourable change in the weather? Are you one of those virtuous folk who write to the angling press recommending further delays in the start of the season? "Give the trout a chance to get into condition," they say. "The middle of April is early enough."

If so you are unlike your grandfather. He had no advantage of modern rainproof clothing and yet it was the February Red rather than the Large Spring Olive that specially interested him on his first ventures to the river. If I agree that his zeal was excessive and premature I cannot agree that the beginning of April is too early. Long before opening day my rod is overhauled, reel oiled, and ever hopeful modifications of nymphs and duns are already tied on the latest brand of nylon. Whatever the weather, I'm off to the river on the first available day of the season. I suppose warm and sunny bee-buzzing spring is what I chiefly hope for. On such a day, at precisely half past one, trout and grayling will come on the rise. That's what I expect and it's glorious in prospect.

But what if the weather refuses? What if there is an abrupt return to winter with wet, squally and miserable days? Do you stay at home? I don't. Frequent experience has taught me to rejoice in the prospect of an exciting day at the expense of numbed fingers and eyes blinded with snowflakes. Instead of one thrilling half-hour rise with blank beginning and end to the day, I expect offers at any time and a much heavier bag to carry home at the end.

My earliest recollection of such a beginning to the season was of fly fishing as a boy from the shore of a local reservoir, half of which was private and half public. The bright morning sky soon clouded over and a strong wind sprang up. Then came the snow, heavy and wet. I was forced to retreat to the shelter of pine trees that grew down to the water's edge in the private sector. Before the keeper found me there I had landed five trout and was getting offers at every other cast. The keeper was sympathetic and did not put me off. Perhaps he was too astonished that a boy would persist in such unpleasant conditions. On two succeeding days I returned and in exactly similar weather made similar catches. These were exceptional successes at an early age and left an indelible prejudice in favour of bad weather in spring.

Some springs ago I spent the first week of April on the Tweed. In very mixed weather I had good catches every day, the best times being when the weather got "worse". On those days my flies continued to interest the trout until nearly eight in the evening.

Four springs ago, again on the Tweed, I had five days of terrible weather. I wore consistently two pairs of trousers in my waders and an anorak topped with a gas cape. I kept dry and by my activity quite warm. I enjoyed every bad day of it and have seldom landed so many fish. I say landed, because I returned the largest ones that were too big for my frying pan. It was on this memorable holiday that I first theorised about the why and wherefore of good fishing in bad spring weather.

I noticed that on very cold days the temperature actually rises when the sky clouds over. Rain or even snow, however uncomfortable to the fisher, may be a symptom of this change in temperature which they convey to the water. The dull light which prevails at such times is an additional or alternative explanation. In such light one seldom experiences short rises. Almost every offer is a take. This indicates confidence on the part of the fish, and this confidence may be due to clear vision (which I think is most likely in subdued but evenly filtered light), or else to nymphal activity which stimulates the feeding responses of the trout. I favour the effect of light on the trout rather than on the nymphs. I have used the term "rise" but more often than not the take is an unobserved underwater pull.

What flies are appropriate on such days of wild spring weather? The Large Spring Olive or the Iron Blue Dun are obvious choices. I prefer my own tyings (which change experimentally each year with little obvious effect either way) of the Greenwell and the Gold Ribbed Hare's Ear. The Greenwell is good in any form. But I prefer it as a nymph on a long shank hook, slightly leaded. The Hare's Ear I now make from the fur of my Abyssinian cat. This fly seems to be very attractive to small spring salmon as well as trout. I've hooked one or two every spring in recent years and landed some of them.

Nymph and wet fly, usually well sunk, are best when trout are not showing on the surface: but surprisingly, perhaps, the dry fly can be very successful. It was an early Good Friday when I fished the Tweed near Melrose. The early part of the day, dull but not too cold, gave me enough sport to encourage me to linger. Then, about five o'clock, snow began to fall in huge fluffy flakes that quickly cushioned the whole countryside. They settled on my face and eyelashes so that I had difficulty in seeing. The air was full of them, and as they floated gently down on the water flies began to pop out to meet them and the trout came up in a bubbly rise. I have seldom seen a steadier one. For the next hour, at least, it continued and I took fish after fish, until it was time to make for my bus. That freak blizzard took the whole countryside by surprise. My bus was an hour late; the snow ploughs had to make a path for it; and as I waited I wished I was still at the river, taking advantage of the best spring day I'd ever known: dry-fly fishing in a snow storm! A good Friday indeed!

Oliver Kite records similar experiences: in fact, he designed his Imperial for spring fishing when the Large Spring Olive was up. He sometimes changes its hackle for a freckled partridge one to simulate the March Brown which occasionally lives up to its name and gives sudden flurries of exciting fishing in March. Unlike the Spring Olive, it seems to prefer sunshine and its activity, though spasmodic, seldom occurs late in the day.

So, if spring comes in like winter, don't write to the press about the season starting too soon. Go out and enjoy the good bad weather and the exciting fishing it may bring. If you are concerned about the condition of the trout, you can acquire virtue by returning the big ones to fatten up for the summer. There will be plenty of well-mended medium fish to gladden your heart and your stomach. Be brave and enjoy the inclemency of spring.

[24]

When Trout Refuse the Fly on the Water

For I tell you, Scholar, fishing is an Art—or at least it is an Art to catch fish.　　　　　　　　　　　　　　　IZAAK WALTON

Persistence is not enough. One has to learn. Study, observation, experiment, all play their parts in the progress towards efficiency. One of the fascinating things about fishing is that however much you study, everything has to be *learnt* at the waterside, put to the test of practical experience. Theory excites the intellect, but only practice gets the trout.

Older men are less persistent; or rather, perhaps, are persistent on more selective occasions. Persistence in methods one knows to be inappropriate to the time and circumstances is not sensible— and the older man is usually more knowledgeable about these things. He has less time for useless activity. Nevertheless, the habit of persistency, acquired in earlier years, often tends to operate against reason.

Another factor that prevents the adoption of more reasonable tactics, by blinding the mind's eye to the obvious, is prejudice. My own behaviour on one particular day's fishing is a good illustration of both.

I went to the Clyde, which I have rather neglected in recent years. Below Abington there are some lovely stretches that have often given me good sport.

When I arrived, the complete absence of wind disappointed me. The slower pools and long flats would be difficult or impossible. But it was warm; I could expect some insect activity. It was also very wet—in fact, it scarcely stopped raining all day. That was perhaps why I managed to get a few fish from the smooth water, the raindrops disturbing the surface in much the same way as ripples made by the wind. Most of my fish, however, took in the streamier water. Only two were worth putting in my bag. But it is not the catch I want to record but the sequence of events.

In the early part of the day I fished wet fly down and across, searching the water in the absence of surface indications. I took a few small trout on well-sunk flies. I persisted for about two hours, always hoping for bigger trout. Eventually, I turned about and pitched a leaded nymph upstream. I thought the bigger fish might be nearer the bottom. But the result was the same. By the middle of the day I had returned several more troutlings.

Fishing often improves on a sandwich and a cup of tea. At least, it gives you time to think and look about. I had seen occasional duns fluttering on the stream and had assumed they were Olives. I decided now to make sure. Perhaps a bit of careful observation would be better than persistence in not very successful practice. Leaving my rod on the bank I tried to intercept the flies floating down. There now seemed to be more of them and, what interested me specially, fish were beginning to break the surface.

The duns were coming down and each one seemed to appear suddenly on the surface, as if from nowhere, drift for a very short distance and then take off. Occasionally, one would fail to rise at the first attempt and touch down again momentarily before being fully airborne. None of those I watched remained on the water for more than a few seconds or floated for more than two or three feet. Remember, it was a very wet day, and yet their wings were dry in almost no time.

I failed to catch even a single specimen. A few fluttered off even as my fingers closed on their upright wings. I gave up the attempt to catch one.

The only thing left was to identify them by sight. I bent down with my nose almost touching the water and was lucky enough to get some body views at perhaps a yard's distance. There was no mistaking the olive sheen. But what kind of Olive they were I could not determine, in spite of all my study of Harris and Goddard, though I guessed Medium Olive. It was most humiliating. Perhaps it was the poor light. But two things were certain. Fish were rising ever more frequently and Olive duns were on the surface. That ought to be pretty conclusive. Besides, it suited my prejudices.

I don't nowadays fish dry fly as often as I used, because I've learnt it's not so often the appropriate method. But I'm always glad of an excuse to return to what is still my favourite form of fishing. So I mounted a hackled Greenwell and felt quite confident of a bit of brisk sport to end the day.

I was wrong again. I persisted for two hours during a continuous hatching of flies and splashing of trout. I didn't have a single offer. It was uncanny and I began to feel desperate. I tried every form of Olive in my box, and I have quite a variety.

My resort to trial and error had only one result. It consumed the afternoon and the light was beginning to fail. Obviously the fish were beating me. "I must come to my senses," I said to myself. "There's an answer to all this." So I stopped fishing and watched again.

I could see no change in the facts of the situation, but presently another explanation occurred to me. No doubt anyone reading this account has thought of it long ago and wondered at my stupidity. The trout must be taking some other fly, even though I could see only Olives on the water. Some other small morsels might be invisible in the dull light. But ten minutes later I had to discard this theory, too. All my offerings were being consistently refused.

I had nothing left, unless I used fancy flies, which did not seem suitable to the logic of the circumstances. But by this time I had proved one thing for certain—the trout were not taking the Olive duns. Not a single fly, as I watched, ever ended in the mouth of a trout, and yet trout were still breaking the surface here and there on the stream.

The day was now far spent. I decided to go back down the water towards my car. It was not wisdom, therefore, that decided my last resort. My casting arm was wet from wrist to shoulder and to return to wet-fly fishing for the final half-hour would at least be somwhat more comfortable. I was again faithful to the Greenwell, one with a very sparse hackle but not leaded.

The response was instantaneous. Every cast seemed to raise a trout, though small and not easily hooked. I had solved the mystery by accident. The truth at last dawned on me that the fish all day long had been ignoring the hatched duns in favour of their nymphs.

When the surface rise began it was the hatching nymphs they were after. Perhaps the very brief surface drift of the duns had made it as difficult for the trout, as for me, to catch them, and the trout had shown a wiser conservation of energy. It just wasn't worth the effort to try to intercept them in the brief moment before they were off and away. I had learnt an important lesson after hours of frustration caused by the habit of persistence and the blind spot of prejudice.

In the flush of discovery I wanted to improve the product. Instead of indiscriminate casting, which seemed likely to give me only the ubiquitous fingerling, I now looked for signs of bigger fish and thus, as I mentioned near the beginning, I did manage to get a couple of reasonable ones to take home.

Far more important, however, was the knowledge that I was now equipped by experience to recognise a situation that must be very common. If trout are consistently refusing the fly on the water they may well be feeding on its nymph, either just before, or in the act of, hatching. It seems to have taken me half a lifetime to learn this simple lesson.

[25]

Two Night Experiences

I perceive the fisherman may sometimes be displeased. ANON:
The Arte of Angling, 1577.

Two fishing expeditions last season well exemplify the notorious unpredictability of the sport of fishing. They occurred on successive Friday evenings in August, when I was able to get on to a favourite stretch of the Tweed just before seven o'clock.

The first evening followed a warm sunny day and I had to be careful of my long shadow across the water right up to the time of dusk. The water was low. I took my first trout from a narrow run between long streamers of weed that parted the surface. It took a small dry Badger. After that I continued to catch nice trout until, by about nine o'clock, I must have had half a dozen in my bag and was beginning to think of returning home. But as darkness approached, the rather occasional rises that had given me my opportunities developed into a spectacular evening rise, with heavy fish porpoising in every square yard of the main stream.

I couldn't tear myself away from this chance of a lifetime. But the Badger now ceased to be effective. I removed it, and after five minutes of fumbling with my fingers and straining my eyes in the fading light, I managed at last to put on a tiny fly which I chose for its size, for I was unable to recognise it. During the next ten minutes I cast continuously and got just three offers from at least fifty active trout. I netted two of them, beautiful vigorous leapers that set my heart pounding. By then it was too dark to see the rises. I touched several more fish but failed to hook them.

But I could hear big fish splashing around and moths were brushing my face. Obviously, big night flies were now indicated. I took off the midge and spent a long time tying on a big bushy

N

thing that felt suitable. Holding the hook up to the sky, I could just detect its eye through which, miraculously, I twice succeeded in getting the nylon. The first time, trying to pull it through, I pushed it out and had to start all over again. But after what seemed hours, I was ready, and so were the trout.

From the near bank I cast downstream and a big grayling began a backwards struggle that kept me busy for at least two minutes before I got it to the net. Then, wading up to the edge of the stream, I cast again and was almost immediately taken by a heavy fish that pulled downstream remorselessly and then, by a sudden fling, snapped the cast. That should teach me not to fish night fly on 3 lb breaking strain nylon when big fish are to be expected.

A large full moon rose steadily through a ragged veil of clouds giving a strong light. It enabled me to put on a heavier leader and a new fly which I even thought I could identify, though more by its shape than by its colour—a representation of the cinnamon sedge. During the next hour or so I continued to catch fish every ten to fifteen minutes. One or two I returned to the water, but anything about a pound or over went into the bag. After that the sport came to a full stop. I kept on casting, wondering why the fish I could still hear, and even see, breaking the surface were no longer interested in my sedge.

It was half past two in the morning and the moon was high overhead before I solved the mystery. I found my leader in a hopeless tangle. Suddenly, I felt tired and hungry. I had had a good night. I persuaded myself to pack up. The folks at home might be worrying, for they expected me for late supper, not for breakfast. Before going to bed I laid out seventeen beautiful fish. And I felt very happy in spite of a slight scruple about the ethics of fishmongering.

Throughout the following week I looked forward eagerly to another visit to the river. I made careful preparation. This time my equipment included two meals, several mounted casts, and a torch.

When I arrived I found the water higher because of some mid-week rain. It was no longer broken by the streamers of weed. There was more cloud, though the day had been quite sunny. It was also cooler, with a fair breeze.

Up to the darkening I fished both dry and wet fly and took a few small trout. I kept only one. My wife's parting words had been: "Two good fish are quite enough." No evening rise occurred which I know from experience bodes ill for night fishing. And so it turned out. Though I persisted all night, with two breaks for food, there was no response at all from the inscrutable river. Before dawn it became so cold that I had to stamp about on the bank to mend my circulation. But I still hoped for some success at early light.

A few salmon parr came to small wet flies as the morning gradually brightened, but the trout continued to fast. I wished I had brought worm or spinning tackle. Nothing else seemed of any use. Then I remembered a small fly spoon in a reserve box I seldom use but always carry. I put it on in place of the tail fly. Fly spoons are abominable things to cast with a short rod. I lobbed it out into the shallow, slack water between the bank and the main stream and began to wade after it and cast again, pulling another yard or so of line from the reel. The spoon hadn't even begun to fish, and must have been in the act of sinking, when it was taken by something slow and heavy. The loose line was drawn through the rod rings, to be followed by a steady drain on the reel.

Out there in the heavy water was an irresistible force threatening the 3 lb nylon by which I was connected to it. I had an exhilarating ten minutes after that, at first being played by the fish and only gradually getting control of its behaviour. I hoped it was a large brownie or a sea-trout but soon began to suspect it was a small salmon by the way it performed. It was. Perhaps I was lucky that it wasn't bigger. Again I was made to realise the folly of using fine nylon to heavy tackle. The large hook fell from its mouth when I lifted the fish into the net. A lucky morning after a luckless night.

I went home in time for breakfast without any more fish. What a ridiculous contrast my two captures made, lying side by side on the dish—a 5 lb grilse and a ½ lb trout. But stranger still was the contrast of experience on two successive fishing expeditions.

Three Men in a Boat

I had battled for a week with wind and wave on a diet of milk, eggs, cheese, bere bannocks, and Orkney trout. I was a new man. The heavy oars had lightened daily. Nevertheless, when two strangers arrived with an outboard motor, I thought it an admirable bit of fishing equipment. As there was no other boat, they gladly accepted the invitation to be my guests. The boat sputtered up into the eye of the wind while we discussed position on board and got introduced.

Tom was a school teacher from over the Churchill Barrier. His ambition was to catch "the fish of the week" and win a magazine prize. He was an enthusiast, and easily convinced me that he would achieve his aim.

His companion, Bert, was an Englishman on holiday who had fished for a fortnight and caught nothing. This was his last day, and Tom had promised him success at last. I gave them bow and stern while I sat on on a little plank that bestrode the thwarts.

Presently the engine was silenced and we faced the long stretch of furrowed water. Bert cast first and caught the back of his neck. Not to worry; it happens to the best of us. I unhooked him and gave him some good advice. Then Tom cast. Nothing wrong with that, except that he had a worm at the end instead of a fly. He explained that fly was good in Orkney for the smaller fish, but monsters only came to worm. Interesting news to me, but then I'm always ready to learn.

This Orkney method of worm fishing in a loch seems to differ little from orthodox wet-fly technique. You cast down-wind and raise the rod, or draw in line, as the boat drifts down.

Two variations are possible. You can keep a tight line or, by a quicker retrieve, make the worm swim towards the boat. Though he admitted he'd never seen a worm swimming voluntarily, Tom said he believed the trout were more attracted to an active worm. So he cast a short line and drew his worm towards him.

I made my first cast, a short one. As I raised the rod, there was a flurry at the side of the boat and I was into a fish. First point to fly, a trout of nearly three-quarters.

After that I spent ten minutes recovering Bert's line which was attached somewhere to the keel. He had been watching me dealing with my fish and the boat had overrun it.

Meanwhile, Tom continued to swim his enormous lob, at least a dozen casts, before I was ready again. I let the wind carry my two flies out in front of me. This was intended as a lesson to Bert on how to use the wind rather than any elaborate rod work, which he wasn't proving very good at.

As the tail fly, a black and peacock spider, settled on the water there was a gleam of gold and the line was torn from the reel. It ran for ten yards. Then the fish took to the air. Another run and another aerial caprice before its energy began to diminish. It protested all the way back to the net which Tom held in readiness. A pounder, a very handsome fish.

Bert, too, contributed to the occasion. His three flies were intimately involved with my two within the net. It was all of fifteen minutes later before I managed to unfankle the mess. As a safeguard I reduced his flies to two and reminded him of the "other" rod's duty when a fish is being played towards the boat.

I was very patient about it, perhaps because I had already enjoyed a week's good fishing and a few hours patience was a small price to pay. Meanwhile, Tom had crawled to the stern and restarted the motor. First drift, two fish, both to fly.

The omens were auspicious. The waves had lost their sharp ridges and here and there trout showed in splashy rises which excited our hopes. Even Tom's, for he maintained that worm would still be acceptable during a rise—to big fish, or course.

But the fly scored again. I brought in a half-pounder, rather unceremoniously. "Just a wee thing," said Tom. Then came another, almost double. "Not so bad," said Tom.

I had learnt by this time to steer my captives towards the left, Tom's side, and he was always very competent with the net.

Thus I almost forgot about Bert, whose difficulties were out of my view. But now, there he was, trying to reach the tip of his rod, which a weaver bird had decorated with a nest of line, nylon, and flies.

I grabbed his jacket in time to save him from a header into the loch. He was so apologetic that I felt almost happy while I passed the time unweaving the woof. It is good to help beginners, especially when trout are rising all around. Thus the soul acquires virtue.

At last Tom caught a fish, a fat intermediate specimen, but not a prizewinner in spite of the big worm. "Your time's coming," I said encouragingly. "Numbers are not everything in fishing," he said. "A single fish may be the heaviest catch."

But eventually Tom had to acknowledge defeat—for today at least. He substituted fly for worm and was soon alternating fish with me as the afternoon went by. We finished with fourteen, none of them "fish of the week", but all good trout. Neither of us would claim this a proof of the superiority of fly over bait. Tom has too many experiences the other way to believe that, and I am content to recommend the excellent opportunities in Orkney for fly fishing. Bert's opinions, perhaps, like his fishing, are rather different.

IZAAK WALTON: *The Compleat Angler* (1653). Many editions. Part II by Charles Cotton (1678), more important in respect of trout fly fishing. The Oxford Edition (1960), includes the anonymous *Arte of Angling* (1577), which was perhaps Walton's model.

GEORGE YOUNGER: *River Angling for Salmon and Trout* (1840). My edition is a misbound exasperating copy of the 1864 edition. Younger is very good reading: "The best style the writer can afford from thirty shillings worth of scholastic education." He knew his insects. *Almost* discovered nymph fishing.

W C STEWART: *The Practical Angler* (1857, A & C Black). Many editions. Classic how-to-do-it. Established upstream (wet) fly fishing. Advocated lively "spiders". *Almost* discovered dry fly but set Scots nymphing half a century before Skues.

THOMAS TOD STODDART: *The Art of Angling as Practised in Scotland* (1839), *Angling Songs,* etc. One of my Scottish trio of upstreamers who influenced tradition more than is sometimes acknowledged.

SIR EDWARD GREY: *Fly Fishing* (1899, Dent). One of the best books in the literature of fly fishing.

G E M SKUES: *Minor Tactics of the Chalk Stream* (1910), *The Way of a Trout with a Fly* (1921), *Nymph Fishing for Chalk Stream Trout* (1939, etc, A & C Black). Wonderful reading. Stately Edwardian prose, illuminated by wit and sagacity. Father of nymph fishing.

OLIVER KITE: *Nymph Fishing in Practice* (1963, Jenkins). "Kite's Country" is Wiltshire of the chalk streams but he had experience elsewhere too. Very useful introduction to up-to-date nymphing. Inventor (?) of the "induced take".

CHARLES RITZ: *A Fly Fisher's Life* (new edition 1970, Reinhardt). A modern classic. "High speed, high line" casting technique and many other originalities.

W H LAWRIE: *The Book of the Rough Stream Nymph* (1947, Oliver & Boyd), and other books. Useful introduction for waters that don't come from the chalk. Good recipes for fly tiers new to the job.

T C IVENS: *Still Water Fly Fishing* (1953, Verschoyle). New edition 1970.

JOSCELYN LANE: *Lake and Loch Fishing for Trout* (1954, Seeley, Service). Pioneer book on modern still water fishing. Meticulous instructions on fly dressing (midges, sedges, etc).

C F WALKER: *Lake Flies and their Imitation* (1960, Jenkins). Companion volume to Lane's book. Very valuable dressings.

J R HARRIS: *An Angler's Entomology* (1952 and later, Collins). First modern book on the subjects of recognition and representation. Indispensable.

JOHN GODDARD: *Trout Fly Recognition* (1966), and *Trout Flies of Still Water* (1969, A & C Black). These and Harris's book should be in every serious angler's personal library. The Still Water volume brings us right up to date.

ROGER WOOLLEY: *Modern Trout Fly Dressing* (1932 and later editions, *Fishing Gazette*). Handy pocket book about all kinds of fly dressing except the very latest.

W E FROST and M E BROWN: *The Trout* (1967, Collins). Very complete account of the fish written by scientists, one of whom is a fisher. Not written down to the lay reader but not difficult. A basic book.

Index

Veniard, John, 173
Vertibrate (rod), 81
Vibrations, 29

Waders, 86, 87, 90
Wading, 90, 147
Waistcoat, 87
Walker, C F, 137, 145, 163, 173,
    174, 178, 200
Walker, Richard, 170, 173
Walton, Izaak, 11, 14, 21, 27, 55,
    79, 86, 99, 120, 129, 143, 155,
    158, 172, 185, 189, 199
Waterboatmen, 167, 177, 182
Waterhen Bloa, 127, 130

Wind, 109, 120–123
Window (trout's), 30–2
Wink, 54, 57
Women, 14, 15, 87–8
Woolley, Roger, 200
Worms, 34, 196
Wye, 120

Yellow Broadwing, 177, 181
Yellow Dun, 131
Yellow Halo, 131, 132
Younger, John, 33, 43, 44, 45, 54,
    199

Zulu, 164